# IN HISTORY'S EMBRACE
## Past and Present in Concord, Massachusetts

Rosamund Coolidge, one of the Children of the American Revolution who decorated the graves of Revolutionary soldiers on April 19, 1925.

*From an album of photographs of the 1925 commemoration of the Concord Fight.*

# IN HISTORY'S EMBRACE
## Past and Present in Concord, Massachusetts

Leslie Perrin Wilson

with a foreword by Doris Kearns Goodwin

Library of Congress Cataloging-in-Publication Data

Wilson, Leslie Perrin.
 In history's embrace : past and present in Concord, Massachusetts / Leslie Perrin Wilson ; with a foreword by Doris Kearns Goodwin.
  p. cm.
 ISBN 978-1-884186-42-4 (hardcover : alk. paper)
1. Concord (Mass. : Town)—History—Anecdotes. 2. Concord (Mass.)—History—Anecdotes. 3. Concord (Mass. : Town)—Biography. 4. Concord (Mass. : Town)—Social life and customs—Anecdotes. I. Title.
 F74.C8W55 2007
 974.4'4—dc22
                                        2007016614

Endpaper illustration: Concord Center, looking toward Monument Square, 19th century. *From a card stereograph.*

Hollis Publishing
95 Runnells Bridge Road
Hollis, NH 030419
t: 603-889-4500   f: 603-889-6551
books@hollispublishing.com

# In History's Embrace

*Past and Present in Concord, Massachusetts*

# FOREWORD

Concord has been my home for more than thirty years, and I thought I was reasonably familiar with the history of this special town, where the stirring events of the Revolutionary War remain vitally alive, as do the memories of the illustrious circle of Concord authors who lived and wrote here at the same time—Hawthorne, Thoreau, Emerson, and the Alcotts. So it was that nothing prepared me for how much I would learn from this remarkable book, which relates history the way I wish it could always be taught—through colorful, biographical stories written with drama and telling detail, so that the past is truly brought to life. Moreover, by exploring the tensions Concord has experienced over the years between honoring the past while adapting to the needs of the present, Leslie Perrin Wilson provides valuable lessons for communities far beyond the confines of Concord's embrace.

From the time our three sons were young, the Patriots' Day celebration, complete with the reenactment of the battle at the Old North Bridge, has been one of our favorite events. I can still remember the excited reaction of a child in the crowd as he saw the Minutemen come over the hill to meet the advancing Red Coats. "Here come the good guys," he shouted, to the shared amusement of everyone present. I have long been aware of an ongoing argument between Lexington and Concord as to where the Revolution officially began. Was it on Lexington Green, where the first clash of arms took place, or was it in Concord, where the first British soldiers were killed? What I had not fully appreciated until reading this book, however, was how heated this argument has been over the years, stretching back to the writings of Concord's first historian, Lemuel Shattuck, in 1835.

Most surprising to me was the story that when the United Nations was created in 1945, powerful voices were raised in Congress arguing that Concord would provide a perfect home. The issue divided the town. Some feared its presence would overwhelm and even destroy the character of village life. Others argued that Concord's reputation would be significantly enhanced by the "influx of diplomatic families—'the intellectual cream of the countries of the world.'" In the end, of course, the United Nations settled in the Big Apple.

Within these pages, one compelling story follows another—the legend of the Great Elm tree which served as a "whipping post" for malefactors; the discovery of a legal contract involving a fourteen month old illegitimate boy indentured until the age of twenty-one by his mother to a Concord weaver; the stunning generosity shown by the town when the house of Ralph Waldo Emerson was nearly destroyed by fire; antislavery activities; séances; two sisters drowning themselves in almost the same spot in the Concord River; historic houses being dismantled and moved piece by piece from one location to another.

For me, there was particular interest in the story of William Munroe, son of a pencilmaker, who became a successful businessman and gave the town the public library that remains the heart of Concord's community life. I have loved libraries for as long as I can remember. My first library in Rockville Centre, New York, was, at the time, an old structure with books spilling out at every corner. I can still remember the thrill when I reached the age where I could turn left into the adult room instead of turning right toward the children's section. In those days, each book had a sheet glued to the last page, on which the librarian would stamp the due date and the cardholder's number. It was possible to gauge how many others had read the same book. I liked the thought that the book I was carrying home had been held by countless others; I felt sad for the author when I discovered I was the only one to take a particular book off the shelf. In later years, I wandered through stacks in college and graduate school and, still later, lived in presidential libraries from Austin to Boston, from Hyde Park to Springfield.

Yet, no library has had a greater impact on my life than the Concord Free Public Library, which has become a second home. As I desperately sought a few hours to write when my children were young, its stately reading room provided the perfect escape. Once my boys were in school, I was able to spend both mornings and afternoons there, interrupted only by a friendly librarian carrying a message that my husband was hungry and that it was time to break for lunch. And still, there is pleasure every time I enter the library doors, knowing that Emerson was the keynote speaker at its dedication in 1873. "The real question," Emerson wrote in his journal shortly before the dedication, "is not what you will do with the Library but what it will do with you. You will come here and get books that will open your eyes and your ears and your curiosity and turn you inside out or outside in."

The same could be said for *In History's Embrace*. These superb stories of Concord's past will "open your eyes and your ears and your curiosity," providing a rollicking journey into a treasured New England town.

DORIS KEARNS GOODWIN

February 23, 2007

# PREFACE

Concord, Massachusetts, is, in some ways, captive to its image. As Henry James noted in 1907 in *The American Scene*, the town projects a sense of place all out of proportion to its size and global significance. James's "biggest little place in America" seems to embody New England virtues, culture, and landscape more fully than other towns in the region.

Concord historians have long sought in the town's past compelling evidence of a greater than local importance. They have with justification pointed to its early incorporation and settlement, its influence as the seat of the Middlesex County courts from the late seventeenth to the mid-nineteenth century, its prominence at the outset of the American Revolution, and its role as the home of Emerson, Thoreau, the Alcotts, and Hawthorne. Native son Henry David Thoreau—a critical yet fond observer of Concord—approached the details of the town's gentle landscape, its plant and animal life, and its social history as microcosmic representations of broader truths and larger forces at work. Visitors and tourists—who as a group are crucial to the health of Concord's economy—have responded to the survival of structures and landscapes from various layers in the town's history as the freeze-framing of single, highly meaningful moments in time rather than the evolutionary patchwork that they actually form. And although local people are often more preoccupied with day-to-day issues than with interpreting the past, they are mindful of the historical and literary mythos and the physical charm that draw outsiders to their town and impart prime real estate value to property within its borders. All agree that Concord is special, even unique, in ways definable and indefinable.

Nevertheless, image is distinct from, and not always compatible with, the wheels of political, social, and economic life that keep a town running, promote local values, and meet the needs of the full range of its residents. Thanks in part to Ezra Ripley and Lemuel Shattuck, intense local awareness of the Revolutionary events that set Concord apart from other places with less visible roles in creating the nation was well-established by the mid-nineteenth century. Since that time, if not before, the life of the town has been characterized by intermittent tension over how adequately to acknowledge and to honor the past and to put history to productive use while attending to the business of generating income, allocating resources, accommodating development, incorporating new residents and new cultural influences, educating the young, attending to the disadvantaged in a relatively affluent environment, and maintaining a strong commitment to the New England tradition of local government.

Admirers of Concord from across the country may define the essence of the town as a combination of Revolutionary independence and Transcendental idealism. While the people who live here would not deny the power and perhaps the interrelatedness of these forces, they are more likely to recognize the "uniform good sense" to which Ralph Waldo Emerson referred near the close of his historical discourse at the 1835 celebration of the bicentennial of Concord's incorporation (the first of his many public addresses here) as the single persistent trait which more than any other has made Concord what it is. By this, Emerson meant an enduring respect for both individual and social rights and responsibilities and a pragmatic commitment to working within existing structures and means to ensure expression of "the will of a free and just community."

While Emerson hardly suggested that the system was perfect (he admitted that Concord, like other New England towns, occasionally carried "economy to the verge of a vice"), or that social and political discourse were free from contention, he took care to emphasize that Concord's management of its own affairs had produced "no ridiculous laws, no eaves-dropping legislators, no hanging of witches, no ghosts, no whipping of quakers, no unnatural crimes"—no extremes that grossly subordinated individual rights to apparent community imperatives. Despite the temptation to view the story of Concord in terms of discrete moments of heroism and high idealism standing out from the pedestrian fabric of local events, the spirit of this place has, in fact, been consistently expressed as a hands-on involvement in political and social processes to solve the problems of the moment and to balance conflicting demands.

Another burden of image under which the town's residents have labored—and continue to labor—is the idea that Concord resists change. To some extent, this is true. How could it be otherwise for a place endowed with a larger-than-life historical heritage, an economic investment in that heritage, strong local traditions, and considerable pride—a place that even today, after centuries of diaspora, remains home to more than a few descendants of those who lived here in the seventeenth, eighteenth, and nineteenth centuries? Where the past remains palpable in the present, change may seem undesirable, even threatening. Determining what is worth preserving and what can be yielded to progress may be divisive, and insistence on having one's dissenting opinion heard may be interpreted as evidence of conservatism. But Concord has, in fact, repeatedly faced and adapted to change. Conantum, the town's first large-scale planned residential development, provides a striking example. Built during the 1950s despite considerable local distress over what its unfamiliar architecture would do to the Sudbury River landscape and discomfort with the ethnic and social diversity of the first homebuyers there, the neighborhood recently celebrated its fiftieth anniversary. Over the years, it has become a highly self-aware Concord institution in its own right.

Few people have done as much to document and to promote Concord's history as Ruth Robinson Wheeler, author of *Concord: Climate for Freedom* (first published in 1967). Even as she carefully researched and wrote about the town's past and its historical and architectural treasures, Mrs. Wheeler approached the present moment as part of the continuum of history. Characteristically, in a January 3, 1946 letter to the editor of *The Concord Journal* about the then-raging controversy over the possible location of the United Nations headquarters in Concord, she reminded her fellow townsmen that some had wrongly predicted in 1840 that the railroad would destroy Concord, in 1890 the trolley, in 1910 the automobile, and in 1940 the airport. Whether right or wrong about the United Nations issue, this forward-thinking woman clearly grasped that it is neither practical nor constructive to hold up stasis as an ideal. By and large, her townsmen have shared this understanding. Concord residents are quick to point out that the town is no Colonial Williamsburg or Old Sturbridge Village, but a place where people really live and work.

Difficult as preservation and development issues in particular can be, and intertwined with the question of individual rights, Concordians address them through the same forums for discussion and the same political processes through which they channel other matters that concern the community. The results may not often satisfy all parties, but on the whole they represent trust in the right of individual voices to expression and a sense that it is possible to attain resolution fairly through established means.

This book constitutes an exploration—admittedly partial and undoubtedly highly subjective—of the complexity of Concord history. While some of the component essays do, in fact, deal with widely known people and events, with topics related to the "high spots" of the Revolution and the residence of Transcendental authors here, others focus on relatively unknown themes, on passing issues that just for a moment seemed of paramount importance, on events for which it would be hard to claim a more than local significance. They were written over a five-year period, between 2000 and 2005, and published in *The Concord Journal* as installments of the column "Historic Concord." Of the forty-plus articles that have appeared in the *Journal*, the following twenty have been selected because they most clearly reflect certain recurrent themes suggesting that Concord is more accurately viewed as a work in progress than a shrine: its ongoing endeavors to come to terms with its image; to preserve its past while dealing with the present and looking to the future; to meet its social and civic responsibilities; to define what it means to be a Concordian; and to permit its residents and visitors free expression of the idealism and spirituality that remain constants of human nature but take multiple forms under various circumstances.

Other writers have adopted a more comprehensive and systematic approach, and have done it well. This book is intended not as a final word, but rather as encouragement to expand the canon of topics considered relevant to the meaningful interpretation of Concord history. As caretaker of one of the best local history and literature collections in the country, I am in a unique position to appreciate how much remains to be discovered and written. The Concord that emerges through consideration of a more inclusive subject matter and body of documentation may not bear much resemblance to Henry James's idealized version, but it is, I trust, more interesting. There is no need to make myth from a few strands of a rich and suggestive reality.

LESLIE PERRIN WILSON
*Curator, William Munroe Special Collections*
*Concord Free Public Library*

July 7, 2006

# CHAPTER I

# IMAGE-SHAPING

Concord's tendency to view itself as "the most estimable place in all the world" derives in large part from the more than local impact of the events of April 19, 1775 and the luster of its nineteenth-century authors in the national literary constellation. Because big things have happened in Concord, the town cannot claim an exclusive right to interpret its own history. Nevertheless, even as nationally respected historians and literary scholars have analyzed important chapters in Concord's past, local people and agencies have simultaneously displayed a determination to honor the small as well as the large details of the town's political, social, intellectual, and municipal life, its rich supply of inherited anecdote, its architectural heritage, and the claim of local characters, institutions, and traditions to attention along with the "shot heard round the world" and the legacy of Emerson and his writing contemporaries. Concordians have maintained ownership of their own history by encouraging the expression of multiple local historical voices and points of view on a wide range of topics, and by commemorating their history on their own terms.

The Concord historical community is remarkably decentralized. Concord preserves and interprets its past through a proliferation of privately and publicly managed sites, organizations, and programs, among them the Concord Museum, the Orchard House, the Emerson House, the Old Manse, the Minute Man National Historical Park, the Walden Pond State Reservation, the William Munroe Special Collections of the Concord Free Public Library, the Thoreau Society, the Concord Historical Collaborative (formed for joint programming purposes by a number of these separate entities), the Concord Historical Commission and Historic Districts Commission, and the town-funded oral history project (which since 1976 has provided a vehicle for recording the reminiscences and observations of longtime residents). Concord has to date never appointed an official town historian, has no formal historical society through which to channel inquiries, and endorses no single comprehensive version of its history. The resulting mélange of intersecting, independent interpretations sometimes bewilders those looking for quick answers, but at the same time encourages respect for the many layers that compose the town's historical heritage. Some of Concord's history is national, and some is, in fact, purely local. People connected with the town take interest and pride in all of it, and are unwilling to cede the right to tell their own version of any part of its story, no matter who else wishes to tell it. But pride naturally expresses itself most vigorously in relation to topics of widely acknowledged import.

Concord's pride, like Lexington's, is particularly apparent in its assessment of its great moment in Revolutionary history. When the stakes are as high as credit for national independence, what town does not accentuate its contribution? In addition to pride, secondary factors, too—the need of preservationists to associate the sites they wish to protect with events of recognized significance, for example, and the profit motive as well—have fed into the proclivity to glorify Concord's importance above and beyond that of other places that provided men, money, supplies, strategy, and spirit to the Revolutionary effort. Although it ebbs and flows, local susceptibility to enhancing Concord's role on April 19, 1775 endures, as does the penchant for seeking bits of reflected glory in artifacts and sites to one degree or another linked to the day.

In 1835, in his treatment of the Concord Fight, historian Lemuel Shattuck succumbed to local partiality in his otherwise even-handed history of the town. In 1894, at the town's first official celebration of the newly created Massachusetts Patriots' Day holiday, Ebenezer Rockwood Hoar attempted with only momentary success to heal old wounds created by such chauvinism. In 1925, Concord self-esteem was hurt by the refusal of a famous poet to participate in its local celebration of Patriots' Day. And in the late nineteenth and early twentieth century, the history of the Whipping Post Elm, a local landmark, took on new dimensions through attempts to link it to the Revolution. These few representative stories highlight Concord's alternate impulses to burnish and tweak its historical image and to moderate the excesses that grow out of enlarging the stature of its history and everything associated with it.

## Lemuel Shattuck, Concord's First Historian

Lemuel Shattuck's *A History of the Town of Concord, Middlesex County, Massachusetts, from Its Earliest Settlement to 1832*—the first comprehensive history of Concord—was published by subscription and distributed just after the September 12, 1835 celebration of the two hundredth anniversary of the town's incorporation. Through this volume, Shattuck made a lasting contribution to awareness and understanding of Concord history. Even before publication, the book was mined for information. In preparing the keynote address for the town's bicentennial, Ralph Waldo Emerson borrowed and studied Shattuck's proof sheets. Once published, the work demonstrated to readers in Concord and beyond the advantages of a historical methodology that relied on primary documentation and a variety of data. Simultaneously, it demonstrated Shattuck's awareness that (in the words of his memoirist Charles Hudson, writing for the June 1880 *Proceedings* of the Massachusetts Historical Society) "every municipality constitutes a part of the State, and that some of its institutions belong, as it were, to the State, and that some of the events that occur within its borders form a part of public history." Today, the book remains the starting point for much research on Concord. But despite his overall objectivity, in presenting the Concord Fight Shattuck, like others, was swayed by the impulse to elevate Concord's role in the events of April 19, 1775 above that of other towns.

Born in Ashby, Massachusetts, in 1793, Lemuel Shattuck was raised in New Ipswich, New Hampshire. His formal education was limited to attendance at the local common school and two quarters at Appleton Academy. Driven by native intelligence, curiosity, energy, discipline, and persistence, he was essentially a self-taught man. His first career was as a schoolteacher. He taught for two years in Troy and Albany, New York, and for four years in Detroit, Michigan, where he also organized and ran Michigan's first Sunday school. In 1823, he moved to Concord and joined his older brother Daniel in keeping store in what is now part of the Colonial Inn on Monument Square.

Daniel Shattuck was shrewd, enterprising, genial, witty, and socially adept. The consummate entrepreneur, he took calculated risks that paid off handsomely, ran a thriving store business, and made money through real estate and stock investments. He was an incorporator and treasurer of the Concord Mill Dam Company (a real estate development corporation formed in the 1820s to revitalize downtown Concord) and the first president of the Concord Bank.

Lemuel was cut from different cloth. George Keyes, who wrote a biographical sketch of him for the second series of printed memoirs of members of the Social Circle in Concord (a self-perpetuating men's social club established in the late eighteenth century), described him as "averse to mercantile and professional pursuits, but among books . . . always at home." Keyes was forthright about his studious subject's "very precise and pompous" manner. Not surprisingly, people who sent their children on errands to the Shattuck store told them to deal only with Daniel. But what Lemuel Shattuck lacked in personal charm, he made up for through thoughtful involvement in community life during his ten-year residence here. He helped organize and superintended the Sunday school at the First Parish, and served on Concord's School Committee. He wrote the town's first annual School Committee report in 1830, and later, after leaving Concord, as a member of the Massachusetts legislature in 1838 and 1839 was instrumental in making the preparation of annual school reports mandatory statewide.

The 1835 history grew out of a series of articles that Shattuck wrote for the *Yeoman's Gazette*, a Concord newspaper. The book appeared at a time when Americans were taking stock of the past in forging a sense of local and national identity, and was well received on publication. In April 1836, *The North American Review* ran a piece by B.B. Thatcher, who commended Shattuck for the breadth and depth of his research into local, county, and state records and private papers as well as into previously published material. Moreover, both Thatcher and, later, Charles Hudson extolled Shattuck's vision of Concord history as part of something larger than itself—the broader history of the state and the nation.

The author's organization of his material was also a selling point. Following a multi-chapter chronological section on Concord from settlement to his own time, Shattuck included topical presentations of various aspects of local history—ecclesiastical, natural, topographical, statistical, social, and official—and the history of the surrounding towns of Bedford, Acton, Lincoln, and Carlisle, which all broke off from the original mother town Concord. The topical approach was lauded as an advance over the strictly chronological.

It enhanced ease of reference, encouraged analysis of continuity and change in relation to specific subjects, and was more interesting than the annalistic method. While Shattuck is unlikely ever to be considered a literary stylist (there is no denying that his fact-laden prose is dry), the care that he took to arrange information effectively is apparent even to modern readers.

Charles Hudson found fault only with Shattuck's attempts to assert Concord's primacy on April 19, 1775 and to downplay the parts played by other towns. In his appendix on the Concord Fight, Shattuck broached a subject that might have been left out of his book altogether without loss of essential information—the question of whether the Revolution started in Lexington or Concord. Echoing words publicly proclaimed by Samuel Hoar in 1824, Shattuck stated of Concord, "There was the first forcible resistance,—there the enemy were *first compelled to retreat:* and *there the first British life was taken.*" Hudson, who by and large found Shattuck a reliable historian, had this to say about such commentary: "He was . . . in his appendix led off into a disputed field, where he appeared as the advocate, rather than the historian; and he was in this way involved in controversy . . . in which he added nothing to his reputation as a reliable authority." Researchers today are still mindful of the historian's pronounced bias in relation to the Concord Fight.

In 1834, Shattuck established a bookstore in Cambridge. From 1835 until 1839, when he retired to devote his full efforts to public service, he was a bookseller and publisher in Boston. Although he is best remembered in Concord for his history of the town, he did his most important work in the fields of statistics and public health after he left here—work to which his research in Concord history directly led. While preparing his Concord book, Shattuck had been frustrated by poor record keeping in various towns where he sought birth, marriage, and death information. Later, he became increasingly aware of the importance of vital records in compiling statistics to document aspects of public health. In 1839, he was a founding member of the American Statistical Association. He also worked toward the passage in 1842 of a state law requiring the registration of births, marriages, and deaths. During his second term in the state legislature (1849–1850), he chaired a committee on registration, which further improved the law.

As a member of the Boston City Council from 1837 to 1841, Shattuck pushed for a city census, which, when approved, he was chosen to carry out. The 1845 Boston census was innovative and influential, particularly in its listing of detailed information on each person rather than for head of household alone. Also, Shattuck prepared an analytical introduction to the census, which became standard practice. The end product was far more useful than any previous census for assessing the factors that affected public health. Shattuck was subsequently invited to Washington to advise on the best methodology for the federal census of 1850.

Shattuck's crowning achievement was his advocacy of public health, which evolved naturally from his statistical work. In the 1840s, he recommended and was made a member of the legislative commission established to conduct a sanitary survey of Massachusetts. He wrote the commission's report (*Report of a General Plan for the Promotion of Public and Personal Health . . . of the State*), printed in 1850. This watershed study ultimately led to the establishment of the Massachusetts State Board of Health and affected the management of public health across America. Additionally, Shattuck endeared himself to genealogists by considering the compilation of family history as well as of public statistics. He prepared *A Complete System of Family Registration* (1841), researched a comprehensive genealogy of his own family (*Memorials of the Descendants of William Shattuck*, 1855), and was a founder of the New England Historic Genealogical Society in 1845. Lemuel Shattuck died in 1859. The later naming of the Lemuel Shattuck Hospital in Jamaica Plain for him reflects his recognition as "the father of public health."

Concord's first historian was a contemporary of the New England Transcendentalists. Unlike these radical thinkers, Shattuck approached the improvement of the human condition pragmatically, from within the system, as a collective rather than an individual effort. Although far from radical, he was nonetheless very much a reformer in an age of reform. But despite his progressive approach in matters of documentation, social history, and, ultimately, contemporary social issues, even this historian's historian was unable to resist the lure of shaping image. He concluded the chapter on the Concord Fight in the body of his book by quoting the high-flown rhetoric of Timothy Dwight: "From the plains of Concord will henceforth be dated a change in human affairs, an alteration in the balance of human power, and a new direction in the course of human improvement. Man, from the events which have occurred here, will, in some respects, assume a new character, and experience, in some respects, a new destiny." Major claims, indeed, for a small New England town.

## April 19, 1894: The First Official Patriots' Day

Concord's first major celebration of the Concord Fight of April 19, 1775 took place in 1825. The first observance of Patriots' Day as a legal Massachusetts holiday occurred on April 19, 1894, by proclamation of Governor Frederic T. Greenhalge. Lexington and Concord have traditionally been keenly aware of their importance at the outset of the Revolution. Over time, the distorting lens of local pride has obscured the roots of Patriots' Day in colonial tradition dating back to the seventeenth century, and has fostered a sense of the holiday as belonging more exclusively to Lexington and Concord than Governor Greenhalge and the Massachusetts legislature intended in 1894. As W. DeLoss Love documented in *The Fast and Thanksgiving Days of New England* (1895), Patriots' Day was created partly to offset the abolition of the annual spring Fast Day, which had been observed in Massachusetts since 1694.

Fast and thanksgiving days were kept in England long before the seventeenth century, when English emigrants to America carried the custom across the Atlantic. The early settlers of New England believed that God meted out hardships as punishment for transgressions and blessings as reward for virtuous behavior. Public fast days were proclaimed by civil authority to atone for actions that might displease God and to insure divine good will toward new enterprises, thanksgiving days to express gratitude for blessings received. Initially, Massachusetts fast and thanksgiving days could be proclaimed at any time, as circumstances dictated. In 1694, the colony adopted an annual spring Fast Day, which ultimately led to the phasing out of specially proclaimed fast days. The annual holiday lacked the sense of urgency of the fast days proclaimed in response to particular exigencies—its focus was more on securing God's favor for the coming year than on the crisis of the moment. The spring Fast Day of 1694 was observed on April 19th.

By the mid-nineteenth century, with church and state no longer one in Massachusetts, there was growing opinion that the April Fast Day should be abolished. Church leaders felt that the religious functions of Fast Day were fulfilled by Good Friday as observed by the various denominations. In 1892, a proposal was made to Governor

William E. Russell that a new holiday be established and that the religious purposes of Fast Day be left to Good Friday. Despite the governor's support, the legislature voted against the recommendation. Consequently, Fast Day was observed in Massachusetts one more time, on April 6, 1893.

Seeking to influence public opinion, the Lexington Historical Society lobbied hard for a holiday to celebrate the events of April 19, 1775. In 1894, Governor Greenhalge expressed support for the creation of a new secular holiday. "An Act to abolish Fast Day and to make the Nineteenth Day of April a Legal Holiday" was drawn up (the connection between the abolition of Fast Day and the creation of Patriots' Day could not have been more explicit in its title), passed by the legislature, signed by the governor, and a printed proclamation of Patriots' Day was issued.

The wording of Governor Greenhalge's proclamation was carefully crafted to suggest complex motivation in establishing Patriots' Day. Greenhalge referred to April 19th as a day "rich with historical

Ebenezer Rockwood Hoar in old age.

*From a cabinet card photograph by Alfred Munroe.*

and significant events which are precious in the eyes of patriots." April 19th was not only the day on which the Battles of Lexington and Concord had taken place in 1775, but also the day in 1783 on which "the cessation of the war and the triumph of independence was formally proclaimed" and the day in 1861 on which "the first blood was shed in the war for the Union." Thus, unity as well as liberty was a theme of the holiday. The governor clearly wished to frame Patriots' Day as a holiday for all of Massachusetts, as Fast Day had once been, rather than for Lexington and Concord alone.

The 1894 Patriots' Day speech in Concord was delivered at the First Parish, before an audience that included Governor Greenhalge, by Ebenezer Rockwood Hoar—lawyer, judge, Massachusetts senator, Attorney General of the United States in the cabinet of Republican President Ulysses S. Grant, Concord native and resident. Judge Hoar's remarkable oration was a model expression of the broad meaning and inclusiveness that Governor Greenhalge hoped would characterize celebrations of the new state holiday. The seventy-eight year old Hoar began by recalling the celebrations of the Concord Fight in which he had participated over the years. He went on to state that Patriots' Day had no "exclusive title" to its name, that there were many other patriotic holidays as well, and emphasized its significance as a Massachusetts, not a local, holiday. He urged a permanent end to "all local bickerings and petty jealousies about the share that one or another town or village, or hamlet, had in the events which have given the day its imperishable glory."

Hoar focused on the collaborative nature of colonial action at Lexington and Concord on April 19, 1775, on the stand taken by the colonists as the joint achievement of many Massachusetts towns. He referred specifically to the involvement of Acton, Cambridge, Arlington, Danvers, Woburn, Lincoln, Bedford, Watertown, Roxbury, Groton, Westford, "and the rest," as well as of Lexington and Concord. He pointed out that if circumstances had played out differently, other towns would have filled the roles taken by Lexington and Concord. "It was Massachusetts in arms that day," Hoar proclaimed.

The judge's magnanimity was all the more striking in light of the fact that seventy years earlier, his own father, Squire Samuel Hoar, had fueled the rivalry between Lexington and Concord. In 1824, when the Marquis de Lafayette visited Concord on his tour of the United States, Sam Hoar informed the town's distinguished guest and the crowd gathered to honor him that they stood on the spot where "the first forcible resistance" of the Revolution had been offered. Needless to say, his highly publicized words provoked the people of Lexington and led to lasting bad feeling.

Ebenezer Rockwood Hoar dramatically drew his speech to a close by asking the Sons of the American Revolution in his audience whether membership in their organization on the basis of ancestry was "wise or desirable," whether it was a truly "American idea." He reminded them that the "shot fired at the North Bridge was heard round the world," not just by those assembled to face British troops in 1775. He affirmed that "every citizen of the Commonwealth who prefers honor and public service to selfishness and ease, who loves liberty, and will resist tyranny without counting the personal cost, wherever he was born and of whatever lineage . . . should have a right to call himself, and is, a son of the American Revolution." Stirring words, particularly from a man descended from seventeenth-century English settlers of Massachusetts, whose grandfather had served as a lieutenant of the Lincoln company at the Concord Fight.

Since 1894, Lexington and Concord have repeatedly but only sometimes successfully faced the challenge of maintaining the expansive spirit in which Patriots' Day was established and first celebrated as a state holiday.

## Robert Frost a No-Show in 1925

By all accounts, the 1925 celebration in Concord of the sesquicentennial anniversary of the Concord Fight was a great success. It provided opportunity for local residents to express pride in their town's place in history and for invited guests and visitors to honor Concord's contribution to the establishment of the nation. The weather was uncooperative, as it has often been on Patriots' Day. But citizens of the town refused to allow rain, sleet, and snow to spoil the fruits of more than a year of preparation.

In May of 1924, Congress passed a joint resolution establishing a United States Lexington-Concord Sesquicentennial Commission, appropriating money for use by local committees of arrangements, and facilitating the issue of special commemorative postage stamps and half-dollar coins. Arlington, Boston, Brookline, Cambridge, Medford, and Somerville planned their own local events to complement those in Lexington and Concord. Judge Prescott Keyes chaired the Executive Committee for Concord's celebration, which spanned two days, Sunday, April 19th and Monday, April 20th. The Vice

President of the United States and the Governor of Massachusetts were among the attending officials. On April 19th, some two hundred Children of the American Revolution in colonial costume proceeded to the Main Street and Hill Burying Grounds, where they placed wreaths on the graves of Revolutionary soldiers. There were band concerts in the afternoon at the Concord Free Public Library and in Monument Square, and afternoon and evening addresses at the First Parish and Monument Hall.

April 20th began with a one hundred and fifty gun salute from Nashawtuc Hill. Major General Clarence R. Edwards was Chief Marshal of the parade. A reenactment of the Concord Fight, arranged by historian and author Allen French, took place at the North Bridge. Athletic events, band concerts, and literary exercises followed in the afternoon. The literary exercises at the State Armory featured an oration by the Honorable B. Loring Young, a poem written and read by Percy Mackaye, and speeches by several dignitaries. In the evening, fireworks at the Emerson Playground preceded the concluding concert and ball.

The celebration was extensively covered in the *Concord Enterprise* and in out-of-town papers. The press paid particular attention to the anniversary parade and reenactment. Although the reportage was glowing, however, not everything had turned out as planned. The *Souvenir Programme of Events* printed somewhat in advance of the celebration and the "Final Program" as it appeared in the *Enterprise* for April 15th both listed Robert Frost as the official poet at the literary exercises. Why did Percy Mackaye take Frost's place?

It would have been a feather in Concord's cap had Frost composed and delivered an original poem for the occasion. After many years of slim appreciation for his creative efforts, he was, by 1925, nationally recognized, his reputation as a leading American poet and a voice of New England established. He taught at Amherst College from 1917, with a break from 1921 to 1923 at the University of Michigan. He was an admirer of the work of Emerson and Thoreau. His literary interest in Concord might well have provided him inspiration in writing a poem for the town's celebration.

The Literary Exercises Committee (consisting of Allen French, Samuel Merwin, and Charles Francis Adams) fervently hoped that Frost would agree to participate. But the original records of the 1925 celebration tell a story of optimism, anxiety, and—at last—disappointment.

At a meeting on September 23, 1924, the full celebration committee voted in favor of the literary subcommittee's plan to engage Frost.
The poet was invited, but the records reveal a conspicuous failure on
his part to accept or decline. He kept Concord dangling for months.
At a March 12, 1925 Executive Committee meeting, the Literary
Exercises Committee could only reiterate its hope—nothing more—
that Frost would come. Later in March, as lists of distinguished guests
and their arrival and attendance plans were compiled, French and his
colleagues included Frost's name among those who would be present
on April 20th. On April 14th, at the eleventh hour, Frost declined the
invitation. As is evident from the final typed secretary's report on the
celebration, his response wounded Concord dignity. The only
acknowledgment of Frost in the official account of the literary exercises is the icy comment, "On the 14th of April, the poet who had
been asked to write a poem for the occasion stated his inability to do
so." On April 15th, poet and playwright Percy Mackaye (like Frost,
also a non-Concordian) was asked in his stead. Mackaye wrote and
delivered the poem "April Fire." Although he enjoyed a long literary
career and recognition during his lifetime, in the eyes of posterity
Mackaye's stature does not approach that of Frost. But his generosity
in stepping in at the last minute allowed Concord to save face. Since
the literary exercises were not a focal point of press attention, Frost's
absence in 1925 was not noted in the newspapers.

Frost was undoubtedly impolite in stringing Concord along, and
the Literary Exercises Committee naïve in trusting that he would be
able and willing to commit to the celebration. But whatever the
poet's culpability in this situation, it is not difficult to understand
why Concord's request was low on his list of priorities in the spring
of 1925. He was much in demand as a poet and speaker, and could
not possibly have accepted every invitation he received. Moreover, he
was at the time preoccupied with his impending return to Ann Arbor
later in the year. He also faced a personal crisis that could not have
been foreseen when he was first asked to be the sesquicentennial
poet. His wife Elinor, at the age of fifty-two, was experiencing an
unplanned and difficult pregnancy, which ultimately ended in mis-
carriage. All of this conspired against his taking part in ceremonies
to which he felt no strong connection.

Frost's rebuff of Concord in 1925 was not the town's first disappointment over outside refusal fully to appreciate its importance in
history. In 1835, the committee of arrangements for the bicentennial

celebration of Concord's incorporation hoped to secure a brilliant and well-known keynote speaker. As nineteenth-century Concord social historian Edward Jarvis made clear in handwritten notes in his personal copy of Lemuel Shattuck's *History of the Town of Concord*, Daniel Webster, Edward Everett, and several other worthies were asked one by one to be the orator, and each in turn declined. To Concord's everlasting credit, Ralph Waldo Emerson was finally engaged as the speaker for the 1835 event. Not yet the nationally renowned figure that he would become, Emerson had only just moved to Concord the year before, and bought his home on the Cambridge Turnpike in 1835. His *Nature*—the clarion call of New England Transcendentalism—would not be published until 1836. With time, however, he became the sage of Concord and something close to a New England regional saint, more than vindicating his selection by the 1835 committee and retrospectively imparting particular literary luster to Concord's two hundredth birthday. But in 1925, there was no budding local bard waiting in the wings to take Robert Frost's place.

The story of Concord's 1925 celebration and that of the 1835 bicentennial highlight the occasional disconnect between local self-image and broader appreciation of the town's significance. As surely as they influence the course of history at all levels, politics, personalities, circumstances, agenda, and point of view inevitably color the presentation of and response to it.

## The Whipping Post Elm: A Tree of Mythic Proportions

In 1941, Concord's Tree Warden cropped the massive but failing Monument Square elm known as the Great Elm, Whipping Post Elm, or Town House Elm, and by Henry Thoreau as the Jones Elm, in preparation for taking it down the following spring. This ancient landmark, which stood to the front-left of the Town House when facing the building from the common, had been weakened by the Hurricane of 1938 and by insect damage and was a hazard to passing cars and pedestrians. Menace though the tree had become, however, its passing was mourned. A July 30, 1941 article in the *Concord Enterprise* noted the sorrow of older residents in particular. Nothing was said in this published tribute of the earlier minor controversy over just how much of the tree's story was fact and how much was legend. For a brief time, disagreement on this subject had drawn attention to the sometimes uneasy relationship between history, local pride, and commercial interest.

Following the Civil War, tourism burgeoned in Concord. Visitors came to town by train, rented carriages, and hired guides. Guidebooks were published, establishing the essential Revolutionary and literary stops on the tourist's itinerary. Souvenirs, stereoptic cards, cabinet cards, and later postcards as we now know them were sold on the Mill Dam. Colorful stories like those connected with the Elisha Jones House on Monument Street (the "Bullet-Hole House") and with the Whipping Post Elm took on significance.

In 1906, Josephine Latham Swayne, in her popular *The Story of Concord*, quoted Judge John Shepard Keyes on the subject of the Great Elm. The old tree, Keyes declared, "was the whipping post from 1790 to 1820, and the iron staple, 8 feet above ground, was in plain sight in my boyhood, on the street in front of the tree. To that staple the culprits were tied up and given the 39 lashes, the law being 40 as a maximum for petty offences. The bark has grown over the staple, and almost even the memory of it. The Elm was planted there April 19, 1776, on the first Anniversary of Concord Fight by John Richardson, the baker and hotel-keeper of the town."

Keyes's story varied in one important particular from local tradition about the tree as it had been written up forty years earlier in *The Monitor*, a short-lived Concord publication. The June 21, 1862 *Monitor* included a small piece in which it was stated that the "old elm on Concord Common . . . was set out in its present place a little

Monument Square, ca. 1895, showing Town House and Whipping Post Elm.
*From an Alfred Hosmer cabinet card.*

while before the memorable day of 'Concord Fight' by a barber. A Mr. Richardson . . . happened to be riding by in his baker's cart just in time, stopped and held the tree while the earth was stamped down around it. It has been used by the authorities as a whipping-post." Sometime between 1862 and 1906, perhaps around the time of the 1875 anniversary celebration of the Concord Fight, the Whipping Post Elm had been transformed into a memorial of April 19, 1775. But its metamorphosis didn't stop there.

In the early 1930s, the tree was specifically connected with one of Concord's heroes of the Revolution. In the summer of 1932, souvenirs made from pieces of the "Emerson Elm"—so called because it was said to have been planted by the Reverend William Emerson, grandfather of Concord's famous philosopher, author, and lecturer—were advertised for sale at Richardson Drug and *The Concord Herald* office. At this point, those who knew Concord history and were familiar with its documentation started to wonder how the Whipping Post Elm had become the Emerson Elm. Historian Allen French—whose commitment to the scholarly exploration of Concord's role in the Revolution was expressed in *The Day of Lexington and Concord* (1925), *The First Year of the American Revolution* (1934), and other writings—looked into the evidence that supported the link to William Emerson. His correspondence and notes on the subject provide a fascinating peek into the workings of a respectful but objective historical mind.

In mid-August of 1932, French wrote Joseph Richardson (the town's Tree Warden at the time) for verification of the Revolutionary Emerson's association with the tree, noting that Sarah Bartlett, Librarian of the Concord Free Public Library, had already informed him that no printed statement supported it. He asked Richardson, "Have we here the beginning of a Concord legend?," and concluded, "If this is false antiquarianism, I think we should nail it before it gets too far."

French inquired of Raymond Emerson whether the story of his great-great-grandfather's planting of the elm had been passed down within the Emerson family. Emerson responded in the negative. French also wrote Judge Prescott Keyes (son of John Shepard Keyes), who replied that while he had heard from boyhood that the tree was used as a whipping post, he knew of no Emerson connection with its planting. Moreover, in startling contradiction to his father's printed words, Keyes stated, "Whipping posts were not used as late as his

[William Emerson's] time. The tree must date from a century before his time."

As French gathered information, John H. Moore wrote an article ("The Town House Elm: When and By Whom Planted?"), which appeared on the front page of *The Concord Journal* for August 25, 1932. Moore observed that elms grow slowly, and questioned whether it was possible for a tree planted in 1776 to have attained sufficient girth by 1790 to serve as a whipping post. He quoted James Raymond Simmons, who wrote in 1919 in *Historic Trees of Massachusetts*, "The elm in front of the town hall must have towered above the British army as it halted in the center of the town." Moore's considered opinion was that the Whipping Post Elm "was planted in its present position, or came up there naturally from seed, at least 100 years before 1776." He concluded by questioning the authority on which statements of its planting in 1776 were based. In response, the editor of *The Concord Herald* sputtered indignantly ("Emerson Elm Planted in 1776, Shown by Historical Records," September 1, 1932) that there was "no more authentic authority than Judge Keyes." Without citing a specific source, he asserted that since Keyes's comments had appeared in print, they must be true.

In the meantime, Allen French was still trying to get to the bottom of the matter. He typed up a summary of his thoughts, beginning by admitting the possibility that the tree might have served as a whipping post. But he doubted that it had been planted on the first anniversary of the Concord Fight. Why, he asked himself, would it have been considered appropriate to use a memorial to Concord's glorious day as a place of punishment? Would a young and small tree have been useable for the purpose? And what was the source of J.S. Keyes's pronouncements as printed in the *Herald*? He wrote the editor of the *Herald* for a reference, and received the answer—no more polite than absolutely necessary—that it was Josephine Swayne's book.

Neither Moore, French, nor anyone else who offered an opinion on the subject raised the additional relevant question of why Concordians would even have thought of planting a memorial tree in 1776, when their energies were fully consumed by the Revolution, long before they had any idea what the outcome of war would be.

The evidence strongly suggests that Keyes's dating of the planting of the Whipping Post Elm was inaccurate, and that William Emerson's alleged role in the event was the invention of later Concordians who hoped to capitalize on the tree's mystique. And what about its use as Concord's whipping post? The only honest answer to this question is "Maybe." Stocks, pillory, and whipping post were certainly used by our Puritan predecessors in New England to punish misbehavior, and were typically located centrally, on town commons. It is possible that the Great Elm on Monument Square served a penal purpose. But the fact remains that no primary source documents the tree's planting and use as a whipping post. The town records from the seventeenth through the early nineteenth century are silent on the subject. Furthermore, Prescott Keyes was correct in pointing out to Allen French that the tree was probably no longer used, or at least much used, as a whipping post between 1790 and 1820, when physical punishment fell into disfavor and was replaced by imprisonment.

Whatever the details of its history, the Whipping Post Elm was felled and missed. In the end, the last generation of Concordians to know the tree firsthand valued it primarily not for its history but for the same elemental reason that Thoreau had admired it—because it was an amazing specimen and a marvel of nature. Their sense of loss was heightened by the advance of Dutch elm disease upon Concord in the early 1940s. People knew that many of the majestic elms that defined the character of the local landscape would soon, like the Great Elm, disappear forever.

The Humphrey Hunt House (demolished in 1859).

*From an Allen French lantern slide, made from the original image.*

CHAPTER II

# CHANGE HAPPENS

Visitors to Concord often marvel at how well the town has preserved its architectural heritage and the beauty of its fields, woods,
ponds, and rivers. But passers-through generally have little way of
knowing the degree to which the town's face incorporates elements
from various periods, of just how much has, in fact, changed over
time, and of the effort that has gone into the preservation of features
of Concord's built and natural landscape. Even in a town as acutely
conscious of its historical significance and as sensitive to the past as a
living force as is Concord, the landscape is constantly altered. Local
needs, values, desires, expectations, and ways of doing things evolve,
and forces beyond human control descend unpredictably. From early
times on, buildings have been moved from place to place with surprising frequency, and some—the truly historic as well as the merely old
and tired—have been lost to business and residential improvement.
Undeveloped and developed parcels of land have undergone radical
changes in use. What outsiders see as a pristine historic landscape is,
in reality, a heterogeneous mix. The town's appearance as it was at
any given moment in its past survives intact only in written and visual
documentation, not in the tangible present.

Accommodation to change is no recent phenomenon, but rather
an enduring fact of Concord life. Many hallmarks of the man-made
landscape have come and gone. The mill pond in the center of Concord, constructed not long after Concord's incorporation in the
1600s, was drained in the 1820s as part of a development scheme to
make money for shrewd investors and to invigorate the town's business district. The seventeenth-century Humphrey Hunt House on
Lowell Road, which held intense interest for Thoreau, was taken
down by owner Edmund Hosmer in 1859 because a later house constructed on the same property (the Hunt-Hosmer House) eventually
made the older building superfluous. In 1866, only a few years after
Thoreau's death, the Fitchburg Railroad built an amusement park at

19

Walden Pond, a popular destination for out-of-town day-trippers. Defunct by the turn of the twentieth century, it only temporarily disturbed Concordians who valued the solitude that Thoreau had celebrated in *Walden, or Life in the Woods* (1854). Today, faint traces of its existence survive. During the 1880s, Concord's district schoolhouses were superseded by centralized schools in Concord and West Concord. Some of the abandoned district school buildings were demolished, some remain in use today as components of houses. A number of landmark buildings—among them the Minot House on Lexington Road, the Hastings House at the corner of Main and Walden in Concord Center, the Middlesex Hotel on Monument Square, and the Hunt House on Punkatasset Hill—came down for a variety of reasons at the end of the nineteenth century and the beginning of the twentieth. The introduction of the automobile spurred the replacement of Concord's picturesque wooden bridges with stronger concrete structures soon after. Reformatory Station on the Middlesex Central Railroad (later the Boston and Maine) line was taken down during the construction of Route 2 in the 1930s. During the 1960s, the once elegant Ingraham-Vose House on Walden Street—earlier moved from its original location and converted to use as a storage facility and plumbing shop—was torn down and replaced by a parking area to facilitate business, banking, shopping, recreation, and community life in downtown Concord. During the same period, what was left of Clamshell Hill—a Native American midden on the Sudbury River and a rich source of artifacts for Thoreau and other collectors—made way for Emerson Hospital parking. In 1970, the West Concord Shopping Plaza was built where the Derby farmhouse had long stood.

Even before real estate development accelerated in the twentieth century, Concord took steps to regulate its growth and to preserve its architectural heritage and rural character. The town passed a zoning by-law in 1928, and seven years later established the Hapgood Wright Town Forest. But development in the mid-twentieth century truly galvanized local desire to approach change deliberately. The completion of Route 2 in the 1930s and the opening of Route 128 in 1951 made Concord a convenient residential location for people working in the greater Boston area. The building of Conantum (one hundred houses on one hundred and ninety acres of land) began in 1951. Conceived by W. Rupert McLaurin, with houses designed by architect Carl Koch, Conantum was followed by other developments that rapidly replaced farmland and open space. As increased development began to alter the landscape at an alarming rate, awareness of land use as well as preservation issues intensified. Town bodies like the Historical Commission, the Historic Districts Commission, the Departments of Natural Resources and of Planning and Land Management, and the Concord Land Conservation Trust were formed in response to accelerating encroachments on the historic and natural landscape.

In addition to town efforts, the establishment of federal and state parklands has also boosted the preservation of open space. The nucleus of the Great Meadows National Wildlife Refuge was donated by Concordian Samuel Hoar—great-grandson of the nineteenth-century lawyer by the same name—to the federal government in 1944. The Minute Man National Historical Park, which encompasses historic properties, landscapes, and much undeveloped area, was created in 1959. The Walden Pond State Reservation came under the administration of the Massachusetts Department of Environmental Management in 1975. Private organizations, too, have formed to protect specific parcels of open space and to preserve individual properties like the Thoreau birthplace on Virginia Road and the Barrett Farm on Barrett's Mill Road.

Nevertheless, change continues. The tension between preservation and development has been moderated, but not eliminated. Concordians today face the same challenges in reconciling the demands of past and present that have repeatedly confronted and drawn strong and varied responses from earlier generations. The interpretation of preservation and conservation issues, their urgency, and the definition of acceptable approaches to resolving them are influenced by the priorities and values of the moment, but the issues themselves persist.

Concordians have responded to changing circumstances in multiple ways. They have moved old buildings from one location to another—today, largely a historic preservation measure, but in earlier times a practical matter of economics, which only coincidentally resulted in the preservation of buildings. In 1928, when Albert Y. Gowen recommended making Concord Center more historic by tearing down aging structures and rebuilding in an older, purer style, they grappled with evolving preservation standards and with the complications introduced by commercial considerations. In late 1945 and early 1946, they reacted vigorously to the proposed location of the United Nations in Concord, parties on both sides of the question using the same facts of history to support their viewpoints. For decades in the twentieth century, they struggled first to accept the decimation by natural agents of the prized American elm—a hallmark of the local landscape—and then to find workable ways of offsetting this loss. Such episodes underscore Concord's durable commitment to mediating between past and present.

## A Moving Story

Richard Wheeler—a Concord resident whose family connection with the town extends back to English settlement in the seventeenth century—is fond of quoting his grandfather Wilfrid Wheeler on the most popular winter activities of the nineteenth century. Grandfather Wheeler identified the "favorite winter sport" of Concordians as "moving houses and suing the neighbor." We simply accept the litigiousness of our forebears as the expression of an enduring aspect of human nature. The frequency with which they moved buildings before the advent of gasoline engines and power tools, however, impresses us more.

During the nineteenth century, many Concord buildings were moved from one place to another, sometimes over significant distances, occasionally more than once. Examples of old structures that (to borrow from Thoreau) "travelled a good deal in Concord" include the Edward Bulkeley House on Sudbury Road, believed to have been moved in 1826 from Main Street; the Emeline (or Emmeline) Barrett House on Court Lane, which originally stood on Monument Square, was moved in 1820 to the corner of Monument Street and Court Lane, and later to its present location; the old Concord Academy building on Middle Street, moved from Academy Lane when Middle Street was laid out (1850–1851); the Nathan Brooks House (or Black Horse Tavern) on Hubbard Street, which formerly stood at the intersection of Main Street and Sudbury Road, and was moved in 1872 to allow construction of the Concord Free Public Library; the Thoreau birthplace on Virginia Road, which was moved from its original site next door in 1878; and the Block House on Lowell Road, moved in the winter of 1928–1929 from the present location of the Middlesex Savings Bank on Main Street.

Nowadays, it is often easier and cheaper to raze an old building, haul it to a landfill, and put up a new one in its place than it is to move and recondition it. People sometimes purchase an old house specifically for its lot, with the intention of demolishing it and erecting one more suited to modern needs and wants. But our Yankee predecessors were less willing to tear down buildings that had required a significant investment in materials and labor to construct. Without modern tools, equipment, and techniques, many man-hours were required to accomplish tasks that are far less time-consuming today. In fact, during the nineteenth century, it made good economic sense to move and recycle a building no longer wanted on its original site. In addition to changing economics, the modern complications of telephone and power lines, plumbing connections, heavy traffic, and the necessity of obtaining special permits have all contributed to the present-day disinclination to move old buildings.

The cost of labor in nineteenth-century America was relatively more expensive than elsewhere. David Stevenson, a Scottish civil engineer born in 1815, traveled in the United States and Canada for three months and published his professional observations in 1838 in his *Sketch of the Civil Engineering of North America*. Noting that American laborers earned more than twice the daily wage of their British counterparts, he wrote, "In consequence of the great value of labour, the Americans adopt, with a view to economy, many mechanical expedients, which, in the eyes of British engineers, seem very extraordinary." Chief among these expedients was the moving of houses, to which Stevenson devoted a whole chapter of his book.

In the nineteenth century, buildings might be moved disassembled, partially disassembled, or intact. As John Obed Curtis explains in his *Moving Historic Buildings*, these same methods are still used today to preserve historic buildings from demolition.

Total disassembly involved the dismantling of a structure piece-by-piece. Each piece was marked so that the various elements could be put back together as they had come down. If the building had a foundation, the stones could be marked, removed, and reused, or the building could simply be reconstructed on a new foundation. Total disassembly involved the loss of a building's original plaster and so was not the method of choice when the preservation of interior walls was a priority. It was, however, well suited to the moving of barns, sheds, and other minimally finished buildings. In recent times, at least one antique barn in Concord housed the clearly marked pieces of another old dismantled outbuilding.

From the architectural historian's point of view, total disassembly as a modern preservation technique has merit, even though it involves the destruction of original plaster and mortar. As Curtis points out, the process allows examination and documentation of the various layers of a structure. For example, the dismantling in the summer of 2001 of Concord's Ball/Tarbell/Benson House (formerly on Ball's Hill Road) permitted exploration of how this early house had evolved over time. (The house was disassembled to save it from demolition and will remain in storage until circumstances permit its reconstruction on another site.)

Partial disassembly involved the removal, marking, and transportation of structural components of a building rather than individual pieces. This method was less time- and labor-consuming than total disassembly. In his account of methods of structural moving for preservation purposes, Curtis describes the partial disassembly of a simple braced frame building of one and a half stories. The interior finish work, plaster, lath, and floors are removed first, then the roof. (As with total disassembly, the original plaster is lost in the process.) Non-loadbearing interior walls are handled as discrete units. The four exterior walls and two gables each comprise a separate unit.

There were various methods of transporting an intact building in the nineteenth century, but before it could be moved it first had to be raised up off its original foundation. This was commonly accomplished by the use of screwjacks. Sections of the foundation were removed to allow placement of the screwjacks under the sills. A large building required more screwjacks than did a small one.

Sometimes little complicated engineering beyond the raising of the building off its foundation was necessary. Under the right conditions, sheer animal power could accomplish the rest. The Jones/Channing House on Main Street, for instance, was moved in 1867 from its original Main Street site on a sled pulled by twenty-two yoke of oxen. As Wilfrid Wheeler's comment about the favorite winter pastimes of Concordians suggests, ice and frozen, snowy ground eased the travel of buildings.

Often, however, additional engineering measures were required to transport a building once raised off its foundation. As described in wonderful detail in an anonymous article on moving houses in the *American Agriculturist* for November 1873, one much-used technique was to place the raised structure onto rollers and to move it to its new site over timbers. The rollers consisted of wooden carriages fastened beneath the building's sills (by means of spikes projecting upward from the carriage) with wheels attached to the underside of the carriages. The rollers traveled over heavy wooden timbers placed beneath the raised building. By means of a rope and pulley or capstan arrangement, a team—generally no more than two animals were required—pulled the building along the timbers. As it moved forward, the timbers from behind were taken up and replaced ahead of it. As long as the move was well managed, the interior plaster would remain uncracked throughout. Scotsman David Stevenson marveled at how successfully even houses with items hanging on the walls were moved.

In some cases, a building might be moved by a tongue and groove type of setup rather than on wheels. It would slide over beams with projections that fit upward into grooves in the wooden pieces above, onto which the sills were fastened. The beams were greased to facilitate movement. More complex situations required special preparations, such as the construction of cribwork to manage the moving of a building down a hillside. As time went by, other forms of power besides animals were used for transportation.

The willingness of earlier Concordians to relocate old buildings has allowed us to know firsthand many historic local structures that might have vanished from the built landscape. But even our ancestors did not recycle every building that no longer suited their purposes. The Humphrey Hunt House was among a number of landmark antique buildings taken down in the nineteenth century. In 1859, Edmund Hosmer demolished the house, which stood on his property, beside his residence (the present Hunt-Hosmer House on Lowell Road). Hosmer's friend Henry David Thoreau was fascinated by the Humphrey Hunt House and wrote detailed journal entries about it. When a building is torn down, such documentation becomes crucial to keeping it part of the town's collective memory. But a standing, occupied antique building affords a far more vital appreciation of social and architectural history and a more tangible link between ourselves and previous generations than even the best documentation of a razed structure can provide. The fact that people today sometimes go to considerable expense and trouble to move and renovate old buildings reflects a modern recognition that our architectural heritage holds a significance beyond the merely practical.

## Williamsburg on the Mill Dam: The Gowen Proposal, 1928

The comment "Concord is not Williamsburg"—meaning that it is a vital place where life goes on in old and new buildings alike, not a museum frozen at a single period in time—is a local commonplace. Residents are proud in particular of the small-town New England charm of the Mill Dam, the commercial district of Concord Center.

The Mill Dam's appeal lies in the unplanned juxtaposition of structures and landscapes representing different layers of Concord's history, combined with the bustle of ongoing business in the area. But in the 1920s, the ambience of Main Street was not universally appreciated. A number of local residents were disturbed by the jumble of pre-Civil War and late nineteenth-century structures. Moreover, some of the older buildings had fallen into disrepair, creating fire and safety hazards. Traffic congestion was a growing problem, too.

In 1928, a radical solution to the decline of the Mill Dam was proposed. An article on the front page of the June 14th issue of *The Concord Journal* outlined a project conceived by Albert Y. Gowen, who had bought considerable business property in Concord Center and intended to purchase more. Once he owned all or nearly all of the area, he hoped to take down existing buildings and replace them with new colonial-style structures. He wanted to "preserve to old Concord the appearance of a real New England town in its business district" and to "prevent speculators from constructing any kind of building" they wished "on a purely commercial basis, with no conformity to

Mill Dam, 1925.
*From an album of photographs of the 1925 commemoration of the Concord Fight.*

colonialism, or to any uniform plan." Gowen sought the approval and involvement of Concord people. He proposed the creation of a corporation and the sale of stock to Concordians who wished to invest in the project. The *Journal* reported that several prominent residents, lawyer Samuel Hoar among them, had already expressed support. The paper made its pages available for response.

Who was Albert Younglove Gowen? Although he disingenuously described himself in the annual Concord street lists as a farmer, he was, in fact, a millionaire cement manufacturer, a large shareholder in Standard Oil, and an accomplished yachtsman, educated at St. Paul's School and Harvard. He moved to Concord around 1927 and remained for about a decade. He owned residential properties on Sudbury Road—the Cyrus and Darius Hubbard House and the Abbott Estate complex, which he occupied and maintained with the help of live-in staff—as well as commercial properties in the center of town.

There were clear similarities between the ongoing restoration at Colonial Williamsburg—funded from 1926 by John D. Rockefeller, Jr.—and Gowen's proposal to preserve old Concord by erecting new buildings according to an ideal of colonial architecture. These resemblances were more than coincidental. A piece in the *Concord Enterprise* for October 10, 1928 noted that Gowen "had had a prominent part" in the Williamsburg restoration. Moreover, the architectural firm that drew up his plans for the Mill Dam renovation was none other than Perry, Shaw, and Hepburn, which directed the Williamsburg project. In 1928, both Thomas Mott Shaw and Andrew H. Hepburn were Concord residents, likely to have associated socially as well as professionally with Gowen. The idea of tearing down old buildings and putting up in their stead others inspired by an earlier period may run counter to our current understanding of preservation. To be fair, however, Gowen secured the expertise of some of the most respected preservationists of his time in formulating his plan.

The Mill Dam controversy played itself out on the pages of *The Concord Journal* in June, July, and August 1928. The vigorous efforts of Wentworth Stewart—the paper's founder/editor/publisher—to keep the issue before the public and his thinly veiled approval of the Gowen proposal are striking from a modern vantage point. Given the political climate in 1928, however, it is not so surprising that Stewart might express approval of a plan harnessing private enterprise to the public end of downtown renewal. He had launched the *Journal* in February 1928, near the end of the Republican administration of Calvin Coolidge and before the election of Herbert Hoover, during a period of persistent and misplaced optimism about continued economic prosperity. Nobody questioned the appropriateness of Stewart's masthead identification of the paper as "Republican in Principle" and his listing among his goals "to promote better and larger local business."

In the June 21st issue of the paper, Stewart proclaimed the fact that Gowen was driven by business rather than philanthropic considerations as a point in the man's favor: "One thing which rang clear from Mr. Gowen was that he was in no way posing as a philanthropist. This statement tends toward confidence." Although Stewart maintained in his articles and editorials that he simply wanted to put the facts before the citizens of Concord, his backing of Gowen was nevertheless apparent—so much so that Charles G. Wood wrote a letter to the editor (June 28th) suggesting that a newspaper had no business intruding in such matters.

What were the major reactions pro and con the Mill Dam proposal? Stewart and readers who responded positively to the plan pointed to Gowen's eagerness to include Concord people in the planning process. Already in possession of considerable Mill Dam property, Gowen could, after all, legally do what he pleased without taking local concerns into consideration. The possibility of property ownership by non-Concordians seeking only investment opportunity on the Mill Dam was also raised as an argument in Gowen's favor. At least the man lived in Concord, even if he was a recent transplant. And the corporation he proposed would consist of local people with a vested interest in the community. Also, the aesthetic cohesiveness of a comprehensively designed downtown was presented as preferable to the architectural dissonance that would result if individual property owners renovated or rebuilt one-by-one to suit themselves.

Other supporting arguments included Stewart's claim that the approval of certain "citizens of influence" should carry some weight with the rest of the population, and the likelihood that revamping downtown Concord would stimulate business and tourism. Several Concord developments were cited as evidence of local sympathy with Gowen's aims, among them the proposed construction according to "Colonial ideals" of the Middlesex Savings Bank (designed by Concord architect Harry Little). Some observed that times had changed, that progress couldn't be stopped, and that the historical sentiment ought not be valued more highly than the benefits of rebuilding to reflect new circumstances and possibilities. Finally, Stewart lauded Concord's inherent conservatism but argued that conservatism might defeat its own purposes in this case and that progressiveness was more likely to yield conservative results.

*Journal* readers opposed to Gowen's plan also sent letters to the editor. Some suspected Gowen's motives and his commitment to local merchants and feared that if he came into sole control of the Mill Dam, he would raise rents to an unreasonable level to recoup his investment. Then, too, there was some doubt that the plan as described could be practically implemented, and some criticism that the specifics of the proposal had not been sufficiently spelled out. The disproportionate emphasis on commercialism over the town's atmosphere and traditions was also noted.

Richard J. Eaton and Marion F. Cook defended the historical value of the existing Mill Dam buildings. Eaton went on to declare that the plan's potential to relieve traffic congestion and eliminate fire hazard could be achieved by means other than obliterating the Mill Dam as it existed, and referred to the state's impending Route 2 bypass of downtown Concord. With some historical justification, Cook pointed out that razing the Mill Dam would provide yet another example of the wealthy among Concord's residents taking down local landmarks for their own purposes. The July 5th issue of the *Journal* contained Frank Pierce's "Declaration of Independence"—one property owner's dramatic statement of refusal to fall into step with Gowen. Summoning the "Spirit of Historic Concord" and the events of April 19, 1775, he vowed that Heywood & Pierce property would "remain in the hands of the present owners indefinitely" and concluded with the invocation "God Save Historic Concord."

The Mill Dam tempest died down after the appearance of the *Journal* for August 9th, bubbling up again briefly in October, when Gowen spoke before the Concord Board of Trade. Finally, the December 12, 1929 issue included a front page article titled "Mr. Gowen Withdraws from Milldam." Gowen's inability to acquire sufficient property to make the plan workable was given as the reason, but it is difficult to believe that the stock market crash in October 1929—the beginning of the Great Depression—was not a factor. Gowen divested himself of the parcels he had bought on the Mill Dam and later (around 1937) moved to London.

It is telling that those who expressed an opinion in the *Journal* never drew upon the actual history of the Mill Dam to bolster their positions. Although some who wrote letters to the editor (Eaton and Cook) mistakenly thought that the face of downtown Concord dated back to colonial times, the entire area had, in fact, been completely overhauled beginning in the mid-1820s by the Concord Mill Dam Company, a profit-driven development corporation not unlike that which Albert Gowen proposed a century later. The Mill Dam Company bought up property in the center of Concord, drained the mill pond (created in the seventeenth century by damming the Mill Brook to power the town mill owned by the Reverend Peter Bulkeley), tore down some old buildings, renovated others, and put up new structures that were offered for sale or rent. The pillared Concord Bank building on Main Street was among its innovations.

The renovation of the Mill Dam a hundred years before Gowen came to Concord might have been used by both opponents and proponents of his plan to support their positions. Opponents might have argued that many of the existing Mill Dam buildings were genuine antiques, and that because they had been constructed during an important period of Concord's social and economic history, they were significant. Proponents might have cited the Mill Dam Company's activities as historical precedent for what Gowen wanted to do. In 1928, however, the persistent tendency to think of Concord's historical importance narrowly, primarily in relation to the Revolution and the literary renaissance of the nineteenth century, prevented those who responded to the Mill Dam proposal from using history effectively.

Today, the Mill Dam is part of the local Main Street Historic District, a status that affords it protection from the kind of proposal that Albert Gowen made. But the polarities that emerged in 1928— between preservation and development, conservatism and progressivism, sentiment and practicality, aesthetics and economics, spending and frugality, individual and community, private and public, Concord and non-Concord, wealthy and less so—are still operative forces. The tension resulting from the pull between these polarities lives at the core of community life.

## The United Nations in Concord?: "My How the Fur Flew"

Most Concordians are aware that their local history intersected broader history at the outset of the Revolution and during the nineteenth-century flowering of American literature. Fewer know that

Concord thought it might again assume national and international significance in the 1940s, when it was considered as a possible site for the headquarters of the new United Nations.

The United Nations was established through conferences in 1944 and 1945 at Dumbarton Oaks, Yalta, and San Francisco. Adopted in June 1945, its charter went into effect on October 24th. Even before the organization began its official existence, there was tremendous American interest in the location of its permanent facility. Eager to bring it to Massachusetts, Governor Maurice Tobin formed a committee that traveled to London in December 1945 to present the state's case to the United Nations site committee. Today it seems far-fetched that there was ever thought of situating the United Nations anywhere but Manhattan. In 1945, however, Massachusetts residents had reason to believe that it might make its home here. The site committee sought non-urban places that would not require the displacement of many people, with sufficient acreage to accommodate a large facility and accessibility to transportation and to city advantages.

In the November 15, 1945 issue of *The Concord Journal*, William Walker suggested that Concord was an appropriate location for the United Nations. A short news piece in the December 20, 1945 issue of the *Journal* reported that Edith Nourse Rogers of Lowell, local representative in the United States Congress, was working to convince Washington officials that Concord—"where the first blow for liberty was struck"—was the logical spot for it. This information unleashed a short-lived but intense volley of local reaction in *The Concord Journal* and the *Concord Enterprise*.

Strong responses quickly came from two prominent, longtime Concordians, lawyer Samuel Hoar (descendant of a distinguished line of Concord lawyers and donor to the federal government of land for the Great Meadows National Wildlife Refuge) and historian Allen French. Their letters to *Journal* editor Samuel G. Kent were printed in the December 27th issue of the paper. Hoar expressed alarm that the "juggernaut" of change would crush Concord. The town's atmosphere would be irrevocably altered by the United Nations. There would be no financial benefit in the form of tax revenues, and Concord would be expected to supply services—water, sewer, electricity, schools, road maintenance, police and fire protection. Parking, traffic, and town planning would be problematic. In the time-honored tradition of evoking history in support of opinion, Hoar stated that the Concord Fight of 1775 had been fought to ensure the right of self-government, which was now threatened by the fact that the community at large had not been consulted prior to Mrs. Rogers's advocacy of Concord as a United Nations site.

In relatively few words, Allen French presented a series of opposites that painted the issue starkly. He contrasted local with outside control, old-timers with newcomers, city people with small-town folk, the hustle and bustle of progress with transcendent separateness from worldly values, change with stability. He suggested that the presence of the United Nations would "not merely change Concord" but would, in fact, destroy it, and urged its location rather in some growth-minded suburb or undeveloped area.

By January 1946, the controversy was in full swing. Other residents jumped into the fray. The James J. Mansfield Post of the American Legion publicly favored location of the United Nations in Concord. Stedman Buttrick (whose property by the North Bridge later became part of the Minute Man National Historical Park) was reported to have offered two pieces of land for site purposes. Writing for the January 3rd issue of the *Journal*, Concord historian Ruth Robinson Wheeler criticized fear of change.

Mrs. Wheeler pointed out that the site committee would make its assessment of Concord's suitability regardless of local opinion, that the center of town would remain unaffected, and that the United Nations would not likely depend on municipal services. She saw the growth of Concord as inevitable, and remarked that an influx of diplomatic families—"the intellectual cream of the countries of the world"—would provide some quality control over the future composition of the community. She reminded her fellow citizens that dire predictions had once circulated about the effects on Concord of a number of earlier innovations—the railroad, the trolley, the automobile, the airport. "Concord can be spoiled only by stagnation," she commented. After all, the Concord Fight had been fought by agents of change against those dedicated "to keep the Past upon its throne." In the January 10th issue of the *Journal*, in a letter to the editor beginning "My how the fur flew!," Roland Wells Robbins—Lincoln resident, archaeologist, and excavator of the foundation of Thoreau's Walden cabin—praised Mrs. Wheeler's "sensible summation."

The United Nations dispute raged through January. H.R. Bygrave criticized resistance to change and too Concord-centric a view of the world. Signing himself "Spirit of 1775," Wallace B. Conant stated outright that he didn't want "any international organization" coming to Concord. Artist Mary Ogden Abbott wrote cuttingly of those opposed to locating the United Nations here as reactionaries, Tories, and rejecters of Emersonian humanitarianism. The height of passionate rhetoric was achieved in Gertrude Rideout's poem "The Host," the first verse of which read: "If Jesus came to Concord Town, / We would not let him in, / Because some wise men in our midst / Believe that change is sin."

As quickly as it had descended upon Concord, the controversy disappeared. Late in January, the United Nations delegation visited sites in the northeast. An article in the *Enterprise* for January 24, 1946 reported that an extended area including parts of Sudbury, Marlborough, Lincoln, Wayland, Framingham, Southborough, and Concord had been examined and favorably reviewed by the delegation. By early February, however, it was clear that sites elsewhere were preferred. John D. Rockefeller, Jr. trumped efforts to locate the organization in New England in December 1946, when he offered property in midtown Manhattan for United Nations headquarters.

The really fascinating part of this story lies in the powerful, divergent responses of local residents to the idea of the location of the United Nations here, in their eagerness to speak out publicly on this controversial issue, and in their subsequent ability to carry on civilly with one another once the brouhaha died down.

## Concord's Lost Canopy of Elms

The planting of trees by the roadways has long been an expression of local pride. Like the inhabitants of countless other places, Concord residents have a history of actively beautifying their community by setting out trees along its streets and in public areas. In 1833, for example, local citizens banded together to contribute money and labor to placing trees where everyone could enjoy them. The Concord Ornamental Tree Society was formed in September of that year "to improve the scenery in the public places in this town, by means of ornamental trees, shrubs and shades." Its forty-four founding members—including Daniel Shattuck, Edward Jarvis, Abel Moore, Reuben Brown, Samuel Hoar, William Whiting, Nathan Brooks, Stedman Buttrick, Josiah Bartlett, Ezra Ripley, and John Thoreau (father of Henry David)—were motivated by the knowledge that "a variety and abundance of well arranged . . . trees, not only contribute to the pleasantries, health and comfort of a country village, but enhance the value of property in their vicinity and indicate good taste and refinement."

Photographer Alfred Munroe grew up in Concord and lived on Main Street in his later years. He wrote in his *Concord Out of Door Sketches* (1903) of the aesthetic satisfaction afforded by the trees along the town's roads: "It is certainly quite unnecessary to call the attention of our Concord readers to the attractiveness of our streets. No one I think can walk through them and not admire their general beauty. Look up and down Main street or Monument street or the Lexington road, and every one is ready to exclaim how beautiful they all are! The exquisite grace of the foliage, the overarching branches, the delicate shades of green and the strong contrasts of light and shade, are all very fascinating. One of the most charming of these pictures is to stand at just the right point at the junction of Sudbury and Main streets and look up both streets showing vistas that are always so attractive."

Main Street was lined with elms when Munroe wrote these words. But, as the devastation of the elm tree in the twentieth century demonstrates, the predominance of particular species of trees in any location is changeable and sometimes subject to forces beyond

Main Street lined with elms, late 19th century.
*From a mounted photograph by Alfred Munroe.*

control. Human agency is not always the ultimate influence on the landscape. Nevertheless, Concord made a valiant effort to preserve this highly regarded tree.

Here, as in towns across America, the elm—tall and graceful, with dramatically spreading branches—was beloved as a shade tree and an ornament for the roadways. Henry David Thoreau wrote of the tree in his journal in 1850: "There was reason enough for the first settler's selecting the elm out of all the trees of the forest with which to ornament his villages. It is beautiful alike by sunlight and moonlight, and the most beautiful specimens are not the largest . . . It is become a most villageous tree . . ." Rows of elms on either side of a street frequently interlocked high up to form a canopy above the traffic of the road. Concord's Elm Street—originally laid out as a section of the Union Turnpike—was given its present name in 1854 because of the elms that flanked it.

Early in the twentieth century, Concordians were concerned about the threat to the town's stately elms posed by the elm leaf beetle, which defoliated the trees. If its leaves were devoured for two or three years consecutively, a tree could succumb to the predations of this insect. Storm and hurricane also took their toll. The Hurricane of 1938 destroyed some particularly fine old specimens and weakened others, like the Whipping Post Elm in Monument Square.

No menace to the elms was as great as Dutch elm disease, first identified in the United States around 1930. This biological agent radically changed the familiar landscape of New England towns. Dutch elm disease is caused by a fungus carried by the elm bark beetle. The female beetle burrows egg-laying galleries between the bark and wood of dead or weakened elm trees. The galleries foster the growth of fungal spores, which are carried from the tree when the young beetles emerge through the bark, and are transported to the healthy trees on which the insects feed. The spores proliferate in and block the trees' water-carrying vessels, causing damage and creating susceptibility to the burrowing beetles. Some varieties of elms—in particular, the American elm—are more vulnerable to Dutch elm disease than others.

A federal program to control the destruction of elms by the imported Dutch elm disease was implemented in the late 1930s and early 1940s. While it reduced the number of infected elms, it could not stem the tide of the disease, which inexorably made its way northward toward Massachusetts from the areas earlier affected by it.

Concord was keenly aware of the approach of the disease. In the 1933 town report, Tree Warden Joseph S. Richardson drew attention to the possibility that it would reach here. In the 1934 town report, the Committee on Dutch Elm Disease—consisting of Richardson, Mary Ogden Abbott, and John A. Brown—reported that the disease had still not hit Massachusetts, and urged the cutting and burning of all dead elms and elm wood. The committee warned, "Once firmly established, it means that our elms will go the way of our chestnuts, of which there are none left."

By 1942, the disease had arrived in Massachusetts. Its progress to Concord was inevitable. Once it took hold here, the town spent considerable thought and energy on attempts to eradicate or at least to control it. Infected trees were cut and disposed of, healthy trees pruned and sprayed with insecticide. During the 1960s, the town sent samples to the University of Massachusetts under a formal elm tree sampling program. Diseased trees were cut down based on laboratory results. But the infection and loss of elms continued.

In the 1970s, the town sought an improved program to deal with Dutch elm disease. In 1975, a more aggressive application of insecticide was initiated. In 1978, the tactics against the elm bark beetle and the disease it spread were changed. Trees were targeted for control efforts selectively rather than comprehensively. Today, the fight to preserve the species of elm that formerly graced the town has been transformed into experimentation with elm varieties more resistant than the American elm to Dutch elm disease. Despite vigorous intervention at various levels of government, only a few handsome specimens of what was once a large and thriving population of American elms remain in Concord.

# CHAPTER III

# A VIGOROUS COMMUNITY SPIRIT

Even in a place where history looms large, the welfare of residents and quality of community life form the primary focus of local attention and resources. A town's expression of these concerns roughly corresponds to what we think of as community spirit. From the outset, Concord has looked after its own, aiding those in need of assistance through both public and private efforts. In this it is hardly unique. Hands-on involvement is characteristic of small towns. But—Henry James aside—by Massachusetts standards, Concord is no longer a small town. The fact that many present-day residents assert that it is, however, suggests that here, at least, the adjective "small-town" has more to do with opportunity for personal investment in community than with size.

Today, at a time of state and federal administration of many public services, it is easy to forget that welfare functions were once largely local matters. Social responsibility was expressed in a variety of ways, among them private arrangements between neighbor and neighbor, municipal expenditures on residents of the poor farm, philanthropy by private charities like the Concord Female Charitable Society, and organized private efforts toward common causes, such as the work of the Concord Soldiers' Aid Society during the Civil War.

The same mix of public and private commitment that has characterized welfare efforts has also informed Concord's civic and cultural life. Official town celebrations (among them the 1835 bicentennial of the town's incorporation) have been underwritten by private contributions. The Concord Lyceum, a privately managed organization that drew upon the talents of many local people, edified and entertained the town at large in venues private and public for almost a century beginning in 1828. Concord citizens pitched in to landscape Sleepy Hollow Cemetery in the 1850s, lending their personal efforts to the beautification of a public treasure. The Hunt Gymnasium (now known as the Hunt Recreation Center) on Stow Street, a public resource, was built in large part through a bequest to the town by Punkatasset farmer William Henry Hunt.

Now a town of fifteen thousand five hundred people, Concord still holds an open town meeting, a democratic inheritance from colonial times, based on the right and responsibility of all voting citizens to participate in dialogue and decision-making about local issues. In his 1835 bicentennial address, Emerson commented on the inclusiveness of Concord's town meeting as a political forum: "In a town-meeting, the roots of society were reached. Here the rich gave counsel, but the poor also . . . and moreover the just and the unjust . . . In this open democracy, every opinion had utterance; every objection, every fact, every acre of land, every bushel of rye, its entire weight . . . Not a complaint occurs in all the volumes of our Records, of any inhabitant being hindered from speaking, or suffering from any violence or usurpation of any class. The negative ballot of a ten shilling freeholder, was as fatal as that of the honored owner of Blood's Farms or Willard's Purchase." The town's citizen body is much larger than it was in its first two centuries, but Concord still allows for the highest degree of individual participation at town meeting. Moreover, multiple boards, committees, and task forces expand the possibilities for direct engagement in shaping policy and addressing problems. Although Concord has been administered by a selectmen-town manager form of government since 1956, there is strong local feeling that the people of the town govern the town.

Concord history is rich in stories that illustrate the ways in which the people here have responded to community needs and enhancements. Some, like that of the widow's thirds of Mary Minot (Henry Thoreau's grandmother) reveal that mechanisms to meet certain situations were simply built into the social and legal structure of earlier times. Other episodes—Concord's Christmas celebration in 1853 and the mobilization of local people following the fire that ravaged Ralph Waldo Emerson's home in 1872, for example—highlight the abiding impulse to perpetuate community cohesiveness in very personal ways. Still others, like the 1873 establishment of the Concord Free Public Library, reveal the complex interplay of private and public in life here. Concord's community spirit may not be unique, but it is an enduring, elemental strength, and one of the major attractions of residence in this place. Local pride in the town's history coexists with and undoubtedly influences this spirit, but the two operate on separate planes.

## Mary Minot's "Widow's Thirds"

Prior to the twentieth century, a woman's security and status hinged largely on the success or failure of the men in her life, particularly her husband. Under such circumstances, widowhood could be an economic as well as a personal catastrophe. Lacking effective means of self-support and deprived upon marriage of most of the legal rights associated with property ownership, a widow was protected to some extent by the English common law and early American practice of assigning "widow's thirds" (also known as the "right of dower"), which assured her the use of a third of her deceased husband's real estate for life, or until she remarried. (The right generally did not extend to personal property, the ability to own which a woman gave up when she married.) While a man might provide amply for his wife in a will or through other means, she was guaranteed widow's thirds even if her husband died without leaving a will, as was frequently the case. Well into the nineteenth century, in Concord as elsewhere, the right of dower was often all that stood between a widow and homelessness.

Henry David Thoreau was born in 1817 in a farmhouse on Virginia Road, in a room within the widow's thirds of his grandmother, Mary Jones Dunbar Minot (Minott), widow of Captain Jonas Minot. A document drawn up on April 17, 1813 defines the scope of Minot's thirds in detail, specifying the east chamber on the second floor—where her grandson came into the world a few years later—as part of her dower.

Born in 1735, Thoreau's step-grandfather Jonas Minot was a prosperous farmer, a landowner in and beyond Concord, a descendant of seventeenth-century Concord families (Wheeler as well as Minot), a town official (constable and selectman), and an officer during the Revolution. In 1759, he married Mary Hall, with whom he had nine children. The first Mrs. Minot died in 1792. In 1798, Jonas Minot took as his second wife the fifty year old widow Mary Jones Dunbar of Keene, New Hampshire. The new Mrs. Minot brought to the Virginia Road household the children of her first marriage to the Reverend Asa Dunbar, who died in 1787. Her young daughter Cynthia Dunbar—born just before her father's death, later the wife of John Thoreau and mother of Henry David Thoreau—thus spent a significant part of her early life on the Minot farm.

Jonas Minot died on March 20, 1813, leaving Mary Jones Dunbar Minot once again a widow. The boundaries of her widow's thirds were established less than a month later. They were recorded with minute precision, revealing the preference of our predecessors to trust in agreements and contracts in clarifying potentially ambiguous property situations. In this, the Minot dower document is similar to many others like it, which often not only specify the demarcation between the widow's and the heirs' portions of house, barn, outbuildings, and land, but also spell out the rights of way permitted the various parties and any other privileges (use of hearth, oven, well, and sink, for example) accorded the widow.

Old documents characteristically describe property in terms of landscape features which have long since lost their familiarity. The land that was Mary Minot's to use was defined in relation to "the Mill yard . . . Road across the Meadow to Reuben Browns land . . .

Doorway of Thoreau's birthplace on Virginia Road, late 19th century.

*From a mounted photograph by Alfred Hosmer.*

the ditch to land late of Capt. Stephen Jones . . . land of Capt. Bates
. . . the onion garden-meadow . . . land of Wm. Mercer . . . land formerly of Eben[eze]r Stow . . . land of Mather Howard . . . the fence
at the top of the hill . . . the brook . . . the little orchard so called . . .
the back pasture adjoining the House . . . a stake at the end of the
wall . . . the old barn . . . the top of the great rock . . . the new Barn
. . . the bars by the lower well," and so on. The fact that the Jonas
Minot farmhouse was moved to its present location in 1878 from
next door on Virginia Road further complicates understanding of the
exact boundaries delineated.

Leaving nothing to chance, the document explicitly grants Jonas
Minot's heirs the right "to pass and repass with cattle teams and otherwise through said bars by the lower well" and to traverse in the
course of normal farm operations (carting dung and watering cattle,
for instance) other areas designated for the use of Mary Minot. The
Widow Minot was assigned the "front room & chamber & Garret
over it in the east end of the House and one half of the front entry in
common and the bed room in the north westward of the House and
the celler under the front room as far north as the celler window then
running west in a parrelel line with the front of the House to the west
side of the celler with a priveledge to pass and repass to it and a priveledge in the kitchen and sinkroom equal to ⅓ part in common." Her
dower included use of the back yard and the well, too, and "one half
of the wood & Chaise house & . . . laying and cutting wood in the
wood yard east of the House the door yard in front and at the west
end of the House." She also had oven privileges and the right to go
out by the back door. Such specificity placed the respective rights of
widow and heirs above the vicissitudes of family relations. Still, it is
unclear how easily enforced a widow's rights were in cases where
there was bad feeling between the parties involved.

After Jonas Minot's death in 1813, his personal property was
auctioned. For whatever reason, Mary Minot chose not to take
advantage of her widow's thirds of his real estate. Perhaps farm life
in a location remote from the village center simply lacked appeal for
a woman of sixty-five. She mortgaged her share of the farm to Josiah
Meriam and rented and lived in part of a house on Lexington Road.
She later repaid the mortgage, which allowed her daughter Cynthia,
son-in-law John, and their growing family to move into the farmhouse. But John Thoreau found it difficult to farm on the outskirts
of Concord simultaneously with keeping store in the town center. In

March of 1818, when Henry David—or David Henry, as he was named—was eight months old, the Thoreaus left Virginia Road, and rented another part of the house where Mary Minot then lived. They remained there for a short time before moving to Chelmsford. Not long after they left Virginia Road, the farmhouse was sold to settle Jonas Minot's estate.

Perhaps not coincidentally, Mary Minot's grandson would later use the concept of widow's thirds metaphorically in his writings. Thoreau wrote in "Chesuncook" (a chapter of *The Maine Woods*): "These Maine woods differ essentially from ours. There you are never reminded that the wilderness which you are threading is, after all, some villager's familiar wood-lot, some widow's thirds, from which her ancestors have sledded fuel for generations, minutely described in some old deed which is recorded, of which the owner has got a plan too, and old bound-marks may be found every forty rods, if you will search." In relation to the landscape, Thoreau here and elsewhere applied the term "widow's thirds" to suggest neglected areas once cultivated, not genuinely wild, less powerful than true wilderness.

Later in the nineteenth century, women's legal and economic status began to improve. Widows in Massachusetts today fare better than they did in Mary Minot's time. Now when a man dies intestate, his widow is entitled to a larger and more encompassing share of his estate—personal as well as real—than was then standard. But in the nineteenth century, despite their widow's thirds, Mary Minot and many of her contemporaries struggled in widowhood, their dowers insufficient to ensure a tolerable quality of life. In a poignant letter written in 1815, the Reverend Ezra Ripley of the First Parish (then still Concord's only church) solicited financial aid for Mrs. Minot from the Masons. Ripley wrote: "[In] the settlement of the estate of her . . . husband, Jonas Minot . . . she has been peculiarly unfortunate, and become very much straightened in the means of living comfortably; . . . individual friends have been . . . generous, otherwise she must have suffered extremely; . . . being thus reduced, and feeling the weight of cares, of years and of widowhood to be very heavy, after having seen better days, she is induced by the advice of friends, as well as her own exigencies, to apply for aid to the benevolence and charity of the Masonic Fraternity." This letter shows a local willingness to pick up where the law left off in advocating on behalf of vulnerable community members.

## Christmas in Concord, 1853

Nowadays, Christmas overshadows Thanksgiving, which is increasingly regarded as the beginning of the extended Christmas season. The relatively greater importance that we attach to Christmas, however, was not part of New England culture until well into the nineteenth century. Our Puritan predecessors disapproved of Old World Christmas revelry and actively discouraged celebration—even religious observances—of the holiday. Between 1659 and 1681, it was illegal to keep Christmas. Days of thanksgiving, on the other hand, were proclaimed by civil authority from earliest colonial times for the public expression of gratitude. The Puritan suppression of Christmas influenced opinion and behavior for two centuries. Christmas was finally officially recognized as a public holiday in the mid-nineteenth century. But in Concord, as elsewhere in New England, it was slow to take its place along with Thanksgiving as a widely observed celebration.

Looking back in old age on his childhood in Concord in the 1840s and 1850s, William Henry Hunt—a progressive Monument Street farmer descended from generations of Concordians going back to settler William Hunt—recalled the preeminence of Thanksgiving over Christmas in his family. Hunt wrote in his manuscript reminiscences (1926), "Thanksgiving was the great day of the year in that household. Christmas was hardly noticed." Hunt here echoed the words of Senator George Frisbie Hoar, who, in his *A Boy Sixty Years Ago* (1898), referred to Thanksgiving in his boyhood as "the great day of the year."

Although old attitudes changed slowly, by the 1850s Christmas much more clearly resembled the religious, social, and commercial celebration of today than it earlier had. On Christmas Eve in 1853 (a Saturday night), Concord demonstrated through a festive, public display of holiday spirit just how far it had come from its Puritan beginnings. That night, hundreds of people came together at the Town House—then a new building—to spread and to partake of holiday joy. This remarkable event was described in detail in an article written in Concord on December 26, 1853 for *The Commonwealth* (a Boston daily newspaper) and published shortly thereafter under the title "Christmas in Concord." The piece was signed "A.M.W."— probably Anna Maria Whiting, a daughter of Colonel William Whiting, who in 1853 lived on Main Street.

The writer of the piece set the scene in the opening paragraph, describing Concord as "a town, twenty miles from Boston, by the Fitchburg Railroad, famous as the residence of philosophers, poets, and naturalists, and pros and anties of all sorts." Just before six o'clock in the evening, a crowd gathered outside the Town House. When the doors were thrown open, the throng entered and proceeded to the hall within, where a huge Christmas tree, decorated with candles and adorned with presents, graced the stage. (Henry Thoreau wrote in his journal of cutting the tree—a spruce—in the "swamp opposite J. Farmer's.") The ladies of the town stood ready to distribute the gifts. Although it defies belief, the writer claimed that seven hundred children and their teachers formed a semicircle in front of the stage.

In a letter written on December 30, 1853 to Transcendentalist reformer Elizabeth Palmer Peabody, Elizabeth Hoar (daughter of Squire Sam, sister of Ebenezer Rockwood and George Frisbie, fiancée of Ralph Waldo Emerson's brother Charles, who died in 1836, before they could marry) revealed that a listing of the names of all children up to the age of sixteen had been compiled from the school registers. A gift had been readied for each child in town either by family or friends or from a "common stock" assembled over the preceding weeks. The organizers had taken care to match an age-appropriate gift to each child and to tag each present for a specific one. Bundles of clothing had been prepared and money collected for poor families.

As reported in *The Commonwealth*, at six o'clock the crowd joined together in singing a Christmas hymn, following which Saint Nicholas bounded onto the stage, accompanied by tinkling sleigh bells. (A.M.W. so vividly described Saint Nick's rich garb and kindly, mirthful demeanor that the reader wonders which of Concord's citizens filled this starring role.) After Saint Nicholas addressed the assembly, the presents were passed out. As the names were called and the presents handed down, bags of sweets were tossed into the crowd. When necessary to quiet the din and to maintain order, Saint Nick blew his whistle and stamped his foot.

A box had been put together for residents of the poor farm, a collection made for the blind man who sawed wood at the depot and who had six children to feed and clothe. There were presents, too, for some of the more prosperous and well-known among the town's citizens—the good doctor "who has barely survived a martyrdom in the cause of temperance" (Josiah Bartlett, a temperance advocate who practiced medicine in Concord for fifty-seven years); a man whose name "has long since resounded on European shores, and one which his own town-people never hear without an inward tribute of respect and grateful admiration" (Ralph Waldo Emerson, Concord's resident Transcendental philosopher and man of letters); and others as well.

When the packages had all been handed out, the "Carnival of Love" came to an end. Whose idea had it been? A.M.W. identified its originator only in paying anonymous tribute to the "active brain and philanthropic heart of one mother, who wished that every child in town might share the pleasure which yearly rejoiced her own little ones, and who, in the execution of her plans, received ready and efficient aid in all directions." Elizabeth Hoar's letter to Miss Peabody and a letter written by Lidian Emerson to her daughter Ellen on December 11, 1853 both indicate that the public-spirited benefactress was Caroline Downes Brooks Hoar, daughter of Concord lawyer Nathan Brooks and wife of Judge Ebenezer Rockwood Hoar. The Hoars were Main Street neighbors of the Whitings.

In contrast with the abundance of available source material about her high-profile husband, there is relatively little documentation of Caroline Hoar's life, which was essentially private and domestic. Nevertheless, both *The Commonwealth* article describing the community Christmas of 1853 and a 1909 typescript speech by Bessie Keyes Hudson about Mrs. Hoar make clear that, like many other Concordians before and since, Caroline Hoar threw her personal energy and resources without stint and without fanfare into projects for common benefit and enjoyment. Concord's 1853 Christmas festivities reflect the generosity, inclusiveness, and fellow feeling to which Concord's community spirit can rise.

## Fire at the Emerson House, 1872

No other Concord resident has been as locally respected and honored as nineteenth-century philosopher, essayist, lecturer, poet, and sometime minister Ralph Waldo Emerson. Although born and raised in Boston, Emerson's roots in Concord were deep. His ancestry extended back to the town's colonial origins—to Peter Bulkeley, a founder and the first minister of Concord. Emerson's great-grandfather Daniel Bliss and grandfather William Emerson were also ministers of the First Parish, and his father William was born here.

Emerson and his brothers stayed in Concord from time to time during their childhood. The Reverend Ezra Ripley had married their grandmother Phebe Bliss Emerson, widow of Revolutionary minister William Emerson. When in Concord, young Emerson stayed at the Old Manse, Ripley's home and previously that of Emerson's grandfather William. Ripley gave the Emerson boys a knowledge of Concord history and a sense of their ancestors' place in it. Here they experienced small-town life and the pleasures of nature. Ralph Waldo developed a lasting fondness for Concord that in 1834 led him back to settle permanently.

Emerson lost his first wife (Ellen Tucker Emerson) in 1831, resigned from his pastorate at the Second Church in Boston in September of 1832, traveled to Europe in December of that year, and returned to America in 1833 to take up a new career as a lecturer. In 1834, his brother Edward died. Shortly thereafter, Emerson and his mother moved into the Old Manse. There he worked on a book that he had been thinking about for some time. When finally published in 1836, *Nature* would launch his literary career and unleash a period of intense expression of Transcendental thought and reaction to it. In 1835, Emerson bought the house on the Cambridge Turnpike that was his home for the rest of his life, delivered his first public address in Concord at the bicentennial of the town's incorporation, and took as his second wife Lydia Jackson of Plymouth. (He changed her name to Lidian after their marriage.) He brought her back to his new home, which they initially called "Coolidge Castle" after its original owner and later referred to as "Bush."

Although Emerson hadn't been Concord's first choice as keynote speaker for the 1835 celebration, he quickly became the town's most prominent citizen. His Concord heritage and his characteristic humility and inclination to deal kindly with others—no matter what their social status—made local residents feel that he was one of them. In 1837, his "Concord Hymn," written at the request of the town, was sung at the dedication of the Battle Monument near the site of the Old North Bridge. Over the years, he served the town as a Sunday school teacher at the First Parish, through its lyceum, as a member of its School Committee and Library Committee, through attendance at town meetings, and as a public speaker on many occasions.

Those who formed part of Emerson's Transcendental circle were frequent guests at the house on the Cambridge Turnpike. Moreover, unknown visitors from all over often came to Concord just for the opportunity of meeting one of the most recognized men in America. But Concordians knew and appreciated Emerson within the context of town life. Despite the demands made upon him as a public intellectual, Emerson was invested in Concord's day-to-day life. The people of the town responded by accepting him as one of their own—even when his ideas and actions generated controversy, and even though many were quick to admit that they did not comprehend the philosophical issues he pondered. He was an influential man, but he radiated an encompassing sense of democracy that appealed to his Yankee townsmen. "And as a man is equal to the Church and equal to the State," he proclaimed in his lecture "New England Reformers" in 1844, "so he is equal to every other man."

Concord's response to a devastating fire at Bush on July 24, 1872 powerfully demonstrated the depth of local feeling for Emerson. Sleeping on the second floor, Emerson was awakened at half past five in the morning by the crackling of flames and the smell of smoke. He shouted to wake up Lidian (who slept on the first floor), dressed hastily, and ran out into the rainy morning to rouse the neighbors. The town mobilized quickly. The First Parish bell alerted the Fire Department. Sam Staples prevented Lidian from going upstairs to rescue her daughter Ellen's possessions (Ellen was not home at the time), but firefighters and villagers managed to haul a great deal from the burning house. Ellen's piano was removed to the nearby Staples house. Food, clothing, and furniture were saved, as were Emerson's manuscripts (some gathered up by Louisa May Alcott and her sister May) and most of his books. Unfortunately, family papers stored in the attic—where the fire had started—were destroyed, and the house itself was badly damaged.

The manuscript records of Engine Company No. 1 offer no explanation as to how the blaze started. In annotating his father's July 24, 1872 journal entry about the fire (consisting of the two words "House burned"), Emerson's son Edward stated that it was "almost surely" started by the kerosene lamp of a newly hired domestic "prowling" in the attic at night. The July 25th issue of the *Boston Daily Advertiser* suggested another cause: "It is supposed that the fire originated in a defective flue, that it caught on Tuesday morning and had been smouldering ever since."

Despite equipment problems (specifically, a shortage of functioning hose), Concord firemen had taken significant risks to save what they could of the Emersons' effects. The family appreciated what they had done. Emerson wrote a letter to the Fire Department on July 29th to express his thanks for "the able, hearty, and in great part successful exertion in our behalf, in resisting and extinguishing the fire, which threatened to destroy my house on Wednesday morning last." Lidian, too, was grateful for the kindness shown them by their fellow Concordians. She wrote to a friend, "We have received such warm expressions of kindness from our friends, and have witnessed such disinterested action and brave daring in our town's people, that we feel . . . as if Concord was a large family of personal friends and well-wishers."

After the fire was put out, the Emersons were taken to the Monument Street home of John Shepard Keyes, who invited them to remain for an extended period. They turned down the offer and accepted that of Emerson's kinswoman Elizabeth Ripley, who lived at the Old Manse. With the assistance of Emerson's good friend Judge Ebenezer Rockwood Hoar, space for a study was obtained in the Court House on Monument Square. Emerson's books and papers were taken there so that the dispirited man might continue to write. Francis Cabot Lowell, one of Emerson's Harvard classmates, personally delivered a five thousand dollar check (the gift of himself and several other friends) to offset expenses incurred by the fire. Soon after, Judge Hoar presented Emerson with a gift of more than twice the amount of the first, collected from friends to fund a trip to Egypt. In October, with Ellen as companion, Emerson sailed for England. He visited London, Paris, Florence, Rome, and Egypt, saw his old friend Thomas Carlyle for the final time, and met John Ruskin and Robert Browning.

While her husband and older daughter traveled, Lidian remained behind, first at the Manse, then at the home of her younger daughter Edith Emerson Forbes (Mrs. William H.). In the spring of 1873, she and Edith refurnished Bush, which was restored under the supervision of John Shepard Keyes. The Emerson women aimed to make the house look (in Ellen's words) "just like itself only somewhat spruced up and improved" by the time the travelers returned.

Emerson and Ellen sailed home on the *Olympus*, arriving at the Port of Boston late in May. Concord had planned a surprise welcome for them. Detained by ruse on the ship until the town was ready to receive them, they took the half past two Fitchburg train. Emerson was deeply moved and more than a little confused when he stepped off the train at the Concord Depot and encountered a cheering crowd and ringing bells. A band had been hired, and a welcoming arch built by the gate of Bush. A procession of citizens and schoolchildren escorted four carriages—the final one bearing Emerson, Ellen, and the Forbeses—to the house, where Lidian waited. On their arrival, the accompanying children sang "Home Sweet Home." The town could not have shown its affection in a more emotional way.

Even before the fire, Emerson's strength and mental vigor had been waning. His memory was no longer reliable. From the time of the fire until his death in 1882, he was less and less able to lecture and to write without assistance. His son Edward described his father's decline in his biography *Emerson in Concord*: "His last few years were quiet and happy. Nature gently drew the veil over his eyes; he went to his study and tried to work, accomplished less and less, but did not notice it . . . As his critical sense became dulled, his standard of intellectual performance was less exacting, and this was most fortunate, for he gladly went to any public occasion where he could hear, and nothing would be expected of him." Concord carefully protected the dignity of its resident philosopher as he became a shadow of the man he had been.

An idealist who nevertheless accepted everyday life and human society on their own terms, Emerson derived sustaining strength and comfort from his place in Concord as a community. The warm and mutual feeling between Emerson and Concord affected the town as well. A significant part of the town's appeal today, after all, derives from the fact that it was the chosen home of one of the most influential thinkers of the nineteenth century.

## William Munroe's Concord Free Public Library

The Concord Free Public Library, conceived and underwritten by founding benefactor William Munroe, was dedicated on October 1, 1873. Since its establishment, the library has changed in major ways. Both the collections and the staff size are now approximately twenty-five times what they were when the doors first opened to the public. The building has been through multiple construction projects to increase its shelving capacity and its usefulness to patrons. From a staff of one multitalented librarian—Miss Ellen Frances Whitney—who did everything from A to Z, separate departments have evolved to handle the administration of the library, technical services, reference services, the particular needs of the children and young people of the town, and the research demands of those who seek information on Concord history, life, landscape, literature, and people. And, of course, automation and the World Wide Web have radically changed the way the staff functions and information is accessed. And yet, even as the library has changed there has been a continuing recommitment to the high standards of its founder and the idealistic aims that informed its establishment.

The most remarkable things about William Munroe were his foresight in setting up the Concord Free Public Library in a way that still largely defines how it operates one hundred and thirty years later, his active involvement in shaping the library he founded, and his determination and shrewdness in accomplishing his purpose, even in the face of obstacles.

William Munroe was the first child of Concord cabinetmaker and pencilmaker William Monroe (Munroe) and his wife, Patty Stone Monroe. He was born in Concord in 1806, raised here, and left in his mid-teens to enter the dry goods business in Boston. He later moved to New York, then to London, where he remained for about two decades before returning to Boston. As a partner in a Boston firm that was a major owner and the selling agent for the Pacific Mills in Lawrence, Massachusetts, Munroe thrived financially. A lifelong bachelor, he retired from business in 1861 and subsequently divided his time between Boston—his legal residence—and his family's home on the corner of Main Street and Academy Lane, where he summered. He lived full-time in Concord during the final year of his life, and died here in 1877, four years after his library opened.

Although Munroe lived away from Concord for most of his adult life, he loved this town and its history. Henry Francis Smith, in his Social Circle memoir of William's brother Alfred, wrote of William: "He was proud of its [Concord's] history and the memorable events which took place here, and, more than all, of the illustrious men who claimed Concord as their home, whose words and deeds have had such a potent influence in shaping the history of the Commonwealth and nation."

Late in life, Munroe sought to express affection for his native town in concrete form. His first thought was to provide in his will for the Concord Town Library—Concord's first public library, established in 1851 in accordance with newly passed Massachusetts public library legislation. But the entirely tax-supported Town Library was a modest operation—at its largest it consisted of seven thousand volumes—and it did not have a building of its own. As time passed, Munroe came to feel that Concord, with its rich historical and literary heritage, deserved something better—a library that would truly reflect the culture and significance of the town. Once Munroe decided to create a new institution instead of beefing up an existing one, he threw himself into every detail of construction and management. No matter was too small for his consideration, and he left nothing to chance.

Looking back on Munroe's interest in building an ambitious library for Concord, it is easy to underestimate the obstacles he faced. From our retrospective point of view, the Concord Free Public Library is an established and respected institution. But in the late 1860s and early 1870s, not everyone here thought it was necessary to replace an existing operation that, after all, worked well enough with a new and fancier and more expensive one. In the process of giving the town the kind of library he thought it should have, Munroe thoughtfully met a number of challenges. To begin with, he knew that the library he envisioned was too big a project to take on by himself. He was aware that he needed personal, financial, and political allies to make the library happen and, once it became a reality, to give useful and valuable items from their personal collections to build it up.

Consequently, he enlisted the assistance of a number of Concord's leading citizens—men who were involved in town politics, who like Munroe loved Concord, and who were willing to contribute both financially and practically to the library project. He cultivated the support of people like Ebenezer Rockwood Hoar, George Merrick Brooks, Henry Francis Smith, and Reuben Rice—all of whom, incidentally, belonged to the Social Circle in Concord. (In fact, it is fair to characterize the young Concord Free Public Library as something of a Social Circle project.) These supporters subsequently became trustees of the Concord Free Public Library or members of the town's Library Committee.

Munroe also understood that it was essential to think about the form of management that would best ensure the growth of the institution he was planning. He was directly responsible for setting up the joint public/private administrative structure by which the library is still governed today. The Concord Free Public Library is, strictly speaking, not entirely a public venture. It is supported by a combination of public and private funding and governed through the mutual efforts of non-profit corporate trustees and a municipal library committee. The Corporation owns and presides over the library buildings (129 Main Street and the Fowler Branch in West Concord) and the endowed funds that provide for them, and holds and maintains valuable manuscripts and books, artwork, some artifacts, and similar materials (what we now know as Special Collections). The town's Library Committee presides over the staff and the expenditure of municipal funding. Both the town and the Corporation contribute to the purchase of books for the circulating and reference collections.

It is a tribute to how well William Munroe's system satisfies the town's needs that the library's administrative structure has never drawn attention to itself. Today, even people who have lived here for decades are sometimes unaware of this public/private partnership, and of the way in which private ownership for public access safeguards the town's documentary heritage. William Munroe envisioned his library as a comprehensive repository for Concord-related materials before there yet was any other local institution devoted to collecting them. Equally important, he also devised a means of effectively ensuring the long-term maintenance and protection of those materials. Concord's manuscripts, archival records, locally significant books, ephemera, and works of art—which Munroe began soliciting for the library before it opened in 1873 and which are now recognized as part of national as well as of local heritage—are not subject to the political and fiscal pressures that sometimes influence library decisions in purely municipal situations elsewhere.

In addition to planning the management structure of his library, Munroe knew that if he wanted to make his dream a reality it was necessary to work within existing political structures—that is, Concord town meeting, Middlesex County government, and the state legislature. He and his cohorts obtained approval for their plans at town meeting. They arranged for certain road improvements connected with the project through the Middlesex County Highway Commissioners. And they formalized the public/private management of the new library by submitting an act of incorporation to the Massachusetts legislature for approval.

Munroe's road improvements to Main Street, in particular, demonstrate the man's considerable political savvy. When William Munroe was planning the Concord Free Public Library, Main Street from the corner of Walden Street down to the intersection with Sudbury Road was considerably narrower than it is now. Also, the corner of Walden Street jutted quite a bit further into Main than it does today. To ease anticipated traffic problems and to open up the view of his new building from the center of town, Munroe wanted to widen Main Street on the south side, from the corner of Walden down to the library site. Needless to say, his plans to alter the approach down Main Street didn't sit well with everyone. But by proceeding deliberately and methodically and through the appropriate channels, Munroe got what he wanted.

At town meeting in November of 1871, a committee of three was appointed to consider the proposal to widen Main Street. The members of this committee were, not coincidentally, Munroe supporters Frederic Hudson, Reuben N. Rice, and Henry F. Smith. William Munroe estimated that it would cost five thousand dollars to widen Main Street. The committee petitioned the Middlesex County Highway Commissioners to help defray the cost. The county agreed to provide two thousand dollars of the total. Munroe pledged to raise a thousand dollars from private contributions. The remainder (two thousand dollars) was appropriated at town meeting on March 25, 1872—but not without some dissension.

The Committee on the Widening of Main Street responded to several criticisms. The cost of the project raised objections, as did the injustice of taxing residents outside the town center for improvements within the center, and the suspicion that the major motivation behind William Munroe's plan was his desire to better display his library building. The committee answered the points one by one, emphasizing that widening the street was necessary to handle increased traffic, that the proposed improvements would benefit all the town's residents (not just those in the center), and that it was perfectly natural for William Munroe to want to show off his generous gift to the town. And so the citizens of Concord voted in favor of Munroe's request. Trees were cut down, buildings moved, and Main Street took on the proportions with which we are all familiar today.

What kind of building did William Munroe put up in 1873 to house the Concord Free Public Library? It was very different from that which stood on the site previously. Munroe bought the major part of what would become the library lot from George M. Brooks in 1869. The house that then stood on it had been a prominent feature of Concord's landscape for more than one hundred and thirty years. It was built around 1740 by James Holden, who kept the Black Horse Tavern there. It served from 1745 until about 1760 as the meeting place of the West Church, which was formed by dissenters from the First Parish during the evangelical ministry of the Reverend Daniel Bliss. From the early 1820s until 1868, it was the home of Lincoln-born Concord lawyer Nathan Brooks and his family. In 1872, it was moved to Hubbard Street to permit construction of the library. George Brooks, son of Nathan Brooks and antislavery activist Mary Merrick Brooks and half-brother of Caroline Brooks Hoar, was born and grew up in the old house at the intersection of Main and Sudbury. He was not only a lawyer (like his father) but also, to some extent, a real estate developer. He was involved in the Hubbard Estate Improvement Company, speculating in the development of Hubbard Street, which is why the Brooks House ended up where it did.

The Brooks House as it stood on its original site was completely in keeping with the other white-painted New England style wooden houses that surrounded it. But William Munroe was looking to erect something distinctive and impressive as well as functional, and did not feel compelled to adhere to a locally familiar style of architecture. He solicited plans from several professionally respected architects, and chose the Boston firm of Snell and Gregerson to design the library. Born and raised in London, George Snell arrived in Boston in 1850, designed several major public and private buildings there, among them the Boston Music Hall (home of the Boston Symphony

William Munroe's Concord Free Public Library, 1873.
*From a cabinet card photograph.*

Orchestra before the construction of Symphony Hall), and in 1860 formed a partnership with another architect named Gregerson.

Snell and Gregerson drew up meticulous plans for William Munroe's Concord Free Public Library. They later wrote up a detailed description of the building, which was included in the commemorative booklet for the library dedication ceremonies on October 1, 1873. Expressing a very Victorian desire to emulate an earlier style of architecture, Snell and Gregerson described their thoughts in designing the library as follows: "In the treatment of the design the architects have . . . adapted the picturesque features of mediaeval architecture to the requirements and mode of construction of the present day." They described the whole as suggesting "a group of buildings rising successively one above another," culminating in a spired tower on the back (or west) side of the building.

It is impossible to look at early photographs of the newly constructed Concord Free Public Library without realizing what an architectural novelty it must have seemed in 1873. Concord was, after all, no urban metropolis. It was still a primarily agricultural town with a population of not much more than two thousand five hundred people and a pronounced local preference for traditional New England simplicity. The Massachusetts Reformatory—Concord's other prominent Victorian brick building of the 1870s—was several years away from being built. William Munroe's Victorian Gothic library building was, in fact, exotic, and naturally attracted notice and comment.

Novel though their building was, however, Snell and Gregerson were not aiming merely to create something different. Like all inspired architects, they had a vision. Photographs of the 1873 library and the architects' description of it—with details of the uplifting rise of the building's line from entrance offices, corridor, and reading room to the higher central gable above the vaulted book room (what we now know as the lobby) to the tower, which stood eighty-five feet from ground to the top of the spire—reveal the sense of intellectual aspiration they were trying to capture. The tower is long gone—it came down in 1917 to make way for stacks on the back of the building—but the impression that Snell and Gregerson meant to convey still survives in the relatively unchanged, high-ceilinged, vaulted, balconied lobby.

In addition to focusing on the aesthetics of the building, in their description Snell and Gregerson also pointed out certain practical features as well—the library's location, accessibility, spaciousness, shelving capacity (it was designed to accommodate thirty-five thousand volumes), its well-lit and "airy" public reading area, furnishings, safety features, and modern conveniences (gas light and furnace heating), all of which had received William Munroe's attention.

Although it took some in town a little time to get used to Concord's Gothic library, the opening of the new building and the expansion of collections and services that followed generated an enormous swell of community pride and support. Ralph Waldo Emerson himself delivered the keynote address at the library's dedication on October 1, 1873 and served on its Library Committee. Throughout the 1870s, many prominent citizens of the town—its intellectual and literary icons as well as its political leaders and affluent citizens—gave freely from their personal collections to enrich the fledgling institution. By 1880, when George Bradford Bartlett's *Concord Guide Book*—the first full-scale guidebook to the town—was published, the Concord Free Public Library had become a local landmark and a must-see for visitors to the town. Just seven years after the library was dedicated, Bartlett wrote: "In its Free Public Library Concord feels a just pride. To the visitor it is one of the first and most attractive points of interest. The Library building, . . . quite picturesque in appearance, is . . . a combination of the old and the modern styles. From every point of view, it strikes the eye most pleasantly, and is a decided ornament to the town." Bartlett continued on for eight and a half pages describing the treasures and attractions of the library. By the time he wrote about William Munroe's gift, the library was well on its way to becoming the recognized temple of New England culture that pilgrims to Concord consider it today, and a center of community life.

Splendid and spacious though the new library was, even William Munroe realized that it would not remain forever sufficient for the needs of a vigorous and growing town. Before he died, he made provisions for its eventual enlargement. In his will, Munroe acknowledged that "another half century of prosperity in New England" would necessitate expansion, and he provided financially for the eventuality. Others augmented the building fund that Munroe had established. In 1875, Munroe had Snell and Gregerson draw up plans for extension. These plans called for two new wings off the rear of the building, one an enlargement of the circulating library area, one an art museum. The spired tower was to be preserved.

Munroe summoned the Corporation and Library Committee to a joint meeting on September 10, 1875. He presented the new plans and then turned them over to the Corporation for future reference. He died a year and a half later.

From a modern vantage point, it may seem odd that Munroe hoped to develop the Concord Free Public Library as a museum as well as a public library. But when the library was dedicated in 1873, the Boston Museum of Fine Arts—which was formed from the Boston Athenaeum art collection—was only three years old. Locally, the Concord Antiquarian Society (now known as the Concord Museum) was not organized until 1886. Munroe consequently saw the library meeting a need not yet definitively satisfied. As time went by, however, specialized regional and local institutions were increasingly devoted to collecting, preserving, and displaying art and material culture, and the library's collecting focus gradually narrowed. Today, only Concord-related art and artifacts that mesh with the library's existing subject strengths and complement other Special Collections holdings are accepted for addition to the collection.

Although the library has not grown exactly as its founder proposed, it has undergone multiple additions and renovations over the years. It was expanded in 1889 (when a school building from Sudbury Road was annexed to the back); in 1917 (when the tower came down to permit the construction of stacks); in the early 1930s (the Frohman, Robb & Little renovation that both enlarged the building and radically changed the style of its exterior from Victorian Gothic to Jeffersonian); in 1938; 1968; 1986 to 1990 (a renovation designed by Perry, Dean, Stahl, and Rogers); and most recently from 2003 to 2005 (under J. Stewart Roberts & Associates). Since the building is not owned by the town, each large-scale renovation project necessarily involves the raising of significant private funds.

People occasionally ask why the Concord Free Public Library was not named after its founder. Certainly his contemporaries and associates recognized and valued William Munroe's disinterested generosity. Henry Francis Smith, for example, wrote: ". . . to him more than any other man must be given the credit of arousing in the people a sense of public spirit that has continued to the present time and contributed in great degree to make the town such a desirable place of residence." Convinced that the final result itself was sufficient testimony to his efforts and contributions, however, Munroe did not feel it necessary to put his name on the library he built. But appropriately, more than a century and a quarter after the library's opening, the 2003–2005 renovation provided the opportunity to name the remarkably transformed Special Collections—now the William Munroe Special Collections—after the library's original benefactor.

# CHAPTER IV

# WHAT MAKES A CONCORDIAN?

Books by Concord authors past and present—the earliest of them the Reverend Peter Bulkeley, whose *Gospel-Covenant* was first published in 1646—line shelf after shelf in the Concord Free Public Library. Visitors are impressed by the number of well-known writers who have made homes in Concord. Local authors point with pride to their books in glass-fronted bookcases, observing that their work resides near that of Emerson, Thoreau, and Louisa May Alcott. The Concord Authors Collection is, however, anything but a vanity collection. It exists to document the intellectual output of people who live and have lived in town. It includes not only books written in Concord, but, for comparative purposes, sometimes also significant work published before or after a writer's residence here.

Given the nature of this collection, it ought to be straightforward to determine who and what has a place in it. Nevertheless, from time to time there have been attempts to circumscribe just who should be considered a Concord author, labored definitions involving how long a writer lived here, whether or not he or she grew up here, whether a particular book was written pre-, during, or post-Concord residence. This perplexity in determining who is entitled to be considered a Concord author reflects the difficulty of answering the broader questions of what it means to be a Concordian, and who remains connected with Concord in the local collective memory after moving away or passing on. Who best represents the qualities associated with the town's self-image? The answer is multifaceted and subject to change.

Concord was settled in the 1630s by English immigrants whose children and children's children intermarried, resulting in a tightly-knit community where a web of family bonds contributed to the concern of one resident for another. In Concord, as in other early towns in the region, the flip side of this cohesion was local unwillingness to take responsibility for those who obviously did not belong to the town. The New England tradition of providing support for the local poor but not for needy outsiders seeking asylum and financial aid played itself out in the form of selective public assistance and sometimes warning out. In the nineteenth century, when the population became more mobile and the influx of new ethnic groups began to alter the composition of the community, those adaptable to local ways were incorporated with relative ease, while those whose customs were more alien remained outside the established power structure and social circle. Within a few generations, however, Irish, Scandinavians, and Italians were assimilated, threatening Yankee dominance.

Concord-born physician, statistician, and social historian Edward Jarvis spent his final years writing down both his memories of the town as he recalled it from his youth and the results of his research into its earlier history. Among his published works, the article "Supposed Decay of Families in New England Disproved by the Experience of the People of Concord, Mass.," which originally appeared in *The New England Historical and Genealogical Register* for October 1884, stands out as a thinly veiled attempt to harness statistical methods to denial of oncoming heterogeneity. For Jarvis and others of his generation, real Concordians were characterized by English ancestry and long family connection with the town. Today, no one would claim that Concord is a remarkably diverse place, but the ethnic uniformity of earlier centuries is gone. Even now, however, when the term "old-timers" encompasses the descendants of the Irish domestics and Italian farm laborers who worried Jarvis, value is still placed on deep roots.

At times, newcomers have been put off by what they perceived as Concord's parochial clannishness. The town's strong sense of itself and its residents' intense engagement with local institutions and traditions have stifled some seeking acceptance on their own terms. In the 1850s, for example, Harriet Hanson Robinson—wife of Concord-born journalist William Stevens Robinson—failed to find her niche here. As a single woman in Lowell in the 1830s, Harriet Hanson was a mill operative and a contributor to the *Lowell Offering*. After marriage, she shared with her husband a principled commitment to the abolition of slavery, and later in life became an ardent promoter of women's rights. From 1854 to 1857, the Robinsons and their children lived in Concord, as renters of the Thoreaus' "Texas House" on Belknap Street. Although her husband loved the town, and although she made friends, belonged to the Concord Female Antislavery Society, and took advantage of the Lyceum, Town Library, and a variety of social events, Harriet Robinson's feelings about Concord were mixed. In a diary entry made the year after moving to Malden, she revealed just how relieved she was to have left: "Concord is a very nice place . . . But it is a dull old place. It is a narrow old place. It is a set old place. It is a snobbish old place. It is an old place full of Antideluvian people and manners . . . The leaves never shake on the trees and the children never cry in the streets . . . The women never go out, and the streets are full of stagnation. It was so still that walking up and down its streets filled me with horror. I used to feel that I must jump up and *holler*, or do something desperate to make a stir. A good place to be born & buried, but a terrible, wearing place for one to live." Concord clearly did not succeed in making a Concordian of Mrs. Robinson.

Harriet Robinson's experience suggests that willingness to appreciate Concord as it sees itself is important to an individual's identification with the town. Sculptor Daniel Chester French was not born here, and spent most of his adult life elsewhere. Nevertheless, he celebrated Concord's accomplishments and people in his work, and was in turn claimed by Concord as a local product. He began his career as a public artist with a commission by the town to create a monument for the 1875 centennial celebration of the Concord Fight—the now iconic minute man statue, which made French's career, gave him good reason for lasting gratitude to Concord, and has ever since been a credit to the foresight of this place. His early work also included portrait busts of a number of locals, among them Ralph Waldo Emerson (a friend of the French family and an early supporter of young Dan's efforts), Simon Brown (editor of *The New England Farmer* and French's uncle by marriage), and Ebenezer Rockwood Hoar. In 1879, French built a studio next to his father's home on Sudbury Road, where he worked as his national reputation grew. Later, he lent his name to the support of art appreciation in Concord as president of the Concord Art Association. Today, he is regarded as one of the town's own, equal in every respect to any native. The combination of his public acknowledgment of Concord's significance and his own outstanding success in his chosen field makes French, for many, an exemplary Concordian.

Although it unquestionably conveys privilege, affluence per se is not acknowledged as a factor in community respect. The historical sense of inclusive democracy that Emerson stressed in his 1835 bicentennial address has discouraged the open equation of money with influence. Nostalgically revisiting the Concord of his early nineteenth-century boyhood, Senator George Frisbie Hoar (a son of Samuel Hoar and brother of Ebenezer Rockwood Hoar) recollected in *A Boy Sixty Years Ago* (1898): "The town was as absolute a democracy, in the best sense of the word, as was ever upon earth. They esteemed each other because of personal character, and not on account of wealth, or social position, or holding office. The poorest boy in town was the equal of the richest in the school and in the playground." No doubt this comment was easier for a member of the elite to make than it would have been for a struggling farmer, but Hoar believed what he wrote.

In recent decades, some residents have expressed concern over skyrocketing real estate prices, which make wealth a prerequisite to residence, endanger the ability of old-timers to stay, and threaten to undermine commitment to traditional values. For the most part, however, money boosts position within the community only when coupled with an inclination to benefit local institutions and initiatives. By and large, Concordians admire civic-mindedness more than any other trait in their fellow townspeople. Since 1962, the annual Honored Citizen Award has encouraged public expression of Concord's regard for volunteer service to the town. Recipients have come from many walks of life, but all share a strong devotion to Concord and a disinterested desire to improve life here.

And yet, however much the people of Concord respect investment in community, they do not demand that all their neighbors serve as models of responsible citizenship. At times, in fact, they have demonstrated a remarkable tolerance for a wide variety of personal eccentricities in others who choose to live here.

Life stories from throughout the town's history reflect the nuances of Concord identity, but provide no single, all-encompassing profile of what makes a Concordian. The mystery of Benjamin Cheney, a little boy indentured in 1699 to serve as an apprentice in Concord, shows that the weight of contractual agreement sometimes overcame the reluctance of colonial residents to take responsibility for outsiders, but did not necessarily guarantee a place in the community for them. The lives here of members of the James family in the nineteenth and twentieth centuries demonstrate the degree to which local residents may overlook idiosyncrasies in those who seek scope in Concord to live as they wish. Having early internalized the local standard of responsibility to community, nineteenth-century farmer William Henry Hunt made the leap from humble circumstances to wealth, and became a model citizen and generous benefactor. On the other hand, well-known music scholar Theodore Baker, Hunt's stepson, left the town without looking back and fell through the cracks of community memory.

## Whatever Happened to Benjamin Cheney?

Antique documents—deeds and agreements in faded ink on yellowed paper—sometimes beckon the researcher to probe into the human element behind formulaic legal language and archaic spelling. A contract dated June 22, 1699 sealing the fate of Benjamin Cheney, a fourteen month old baby, offers one dramatic example of a personal story that begs to be told. The contracting parties were Mercy Page, "formerly of Watertown (of Late a Resident of Charlestown)" and Daniel Pellett, a weaver of Concord. Unable to provide for the child and in "full power to dispose" of him, Page indentured him to Pellett "in the manner of Apprentice" for twenty years minus two months, or until he reached the age of twenty-one. In exchange, Pellett agreed to maintain him for the term of the indenture and to teach him to weave, read, and write. Why would a woman legally bind a young child for what might turn out to be most or even all of his life? And what became of the little boy indentured at such a tender age to Daniel Pellett?

The vital records of Charlestown reveal that Benjamin Cheney, born April 15, 1698, was the illegitimate child of Mercy Page of Watertown and Benjamin Cheney of Cambridge. With no husband to provide long-term support for her son, Page turned to a colonial practice that provided not only the necessities of life but also marketable skills for adulthood—indentured apprenticeship.

As harsh as the separation of a child from his mother might seem from our vantage point, it was not uncommon in the seventeenth and early eighteenth centuries. As David Hackett Fischer notes in *Albion's Seed*, families in Puritan Massachusetts at all social and economic levels sent their children out to be raised in other people's homes. Sometimes they did so in response to a specific exigency, like the death of mother or father. Parents might also send their children out for better educational opportunities, to acquire a trade, or to encourage socialization during the difficult period of adolescence.

Although Benjamin Cheney was young to be indentured, his situation was not remarkably different from that of many children born into stable households, untainted by social stigma.

How did Mercy Page know Daniel Pellett? Henry Bond, in his *Genealogies of the Families and Descendants of the Early Settlers of Watertown* (1855), cited a deed referring to Mercy's parents, Samuel and Hannah, as "of Concord." In fact, Concord vital records show that they were here in March of 1670, when their daughter Mildred was born. Thomas and Mary Dane (or Dean) Pellett—Daniel's parents—were raising their family here at the same time. (Daniel was born in 1668.) There may thus have been a long-standing personal connection between the Pages and the Pelletts.

Records in the Massachusetts Supreme Judicial Court Archives show that Mercy Page and Benjamin Cheney (the father of Page's child) were each brought before the Middlesex Court of General Sessions of the Peace for the crime of fornication. Both got through the ordeal and went on with their lives. Mercy Page married Thomas Ingrem in Watertown in 1703; Cheney married Mary Harbert in Charlestown in 1706.

But what about little Benjamin? Once indentured to Daniel Pellett, he did not leave much of a paper trail. Since there is no documentation indicating otherwise, he appears to have entered the Pellett household as contracted. The lack of a Concord, Watertown, or Charlestown death record suggests that he survived his childhood. As a minor child, with no part in civic life, he does not turn up in Concord town records. When Daniel Pellett left Concord before Benjamin Cheney completed his indenture, the apprentice presumably accompanied his master. There is no marriage or other record to indicate that he lived in Concord after he came of age.

Daniel Pellett's name, on the other hand, is found in multiple Concord records. Although a weaver, he worked at a variety of other jobs to keep his head above water. He was sexton of Concord's meetinghouse and church building, as his father had been before him. The town records show numerous payments to Pellett between 1699 and 1713 for sweeping and maintaining the building and for ringing the bell to call people to worship, town meeting, and court. When the town voted to foot the bills for caring for old William Cooksey, who was "in a low & poor Condition," Daniel Pellett was initially one of several men paid to look after the unfortunate man, and ultimately his sole caretaker. He was also reimbursed for digging Cooksey's grave in 1712 and that of Cooksey's widow in 1713.

Pellett, who apparently never married, owned property and a house on what is now Lexington Road, at the foot of the Hill Burying Ground. (His small seventeenth-century house may survive as an ell on what is known as the Pellett-Barrett House). The Pellett home was built on land that once belonged to Concord founder and minister Peter Bulkeley. This property eventually came into the possession of Thomas Pellett (Daniel's father) through his wife Mary, whose father, Thomas Dane, had title to it. In 1694, Thomas Pellett deeded it to his son Samuel, who sold it to his brother Daniel in 1697. If Daniel Pellett lived in the house, it would also have been the home of Benjamin Cheney. Pellett sold the property to Josiah Blood in 1706, but remained in Concord for some years following.

Daniel Pellett disappears from the town records after 1713. Concord historian Ruth R. Wheeler wrote that he moved to Connecticut. Connecticut marriage records place his nieces Susannah, Abigail, and Mary (daughters of his brother Thomas) in Glastonbury, near Hartford, in 1716, 1718, and 1720. Daniel Pellett may have lived close by.

Benjamin Cheney's indenture would have expired in 1719. Does any Benjamin Cheney of uncertain parentage show up in the Hartford area around 1720? In 1721 a Benjamin Cheney purchased shares in a sawmill in East Hartford. (Possibly significantly, one of those shares was bought of a John Pellett.) Since 1897, when Charles Henry Pope's *The Cheney Genealogy* was published, the East Hartford Cheney has been identified as a Benjamin Cheney born in Newbury, Massachusetts, in 1699. However, even Pope acknowledged that "Not a line of *documentary* evidence has been found to connect the two; but not a trace or clue has been discovered to connect him with any other Cheney family." The great-grandsons of Benjamin Cheney of East Hartford founded a successful silk weaving mill. It is somehow easier to read the 1699 contract between Mercy Page and Daniel Pellett in light of the possibility, however slight, that the little boy whose life it so affected might ultimately have prospered and even founded a dynasty. But whether or not Benjamin Cheney the apprenticed child ended up in East Hartford, his link to Concord was tenuous. He may have lived here, but he was not truly of this place.

## Wilkie, Bob, and Ned: The James Family in Concord

Henry James's appreciation of Concord as expressed in *The American Scene* notwithstanding, three of his close relatives—two brothers and a nephew—knew the reality of the town far more intimately than the novelist, who never lived here. In the early 1860s, Garth Wilkinson (familiarly known as Wilkie) and Robertson (Bob) boarded in Concord and attended Frank Sanborn's school. Bob returned in the mid-1880s and settled here. Bob's son Edward Holton (Ned) also lived here, in his youth and later.

Patriarch Henry James, Sr. was a religious, social, and literary writer and lecturer. He inherited wealth, and was able to devote considerable thought and energy to the education of his five children— William (born in 1842), Henry, Jr. (1843), Garth Wilkinson (1845), Robertson (1846), and Alice (1848). Having struggled for years with doubt about traditional systems of belief, the elder James was drawn to the religious ideas of Swedish mystic Swedenborg and to the utopian social theories of French reformer Fourier. Although not a Transcendentalist, James was a friend of Ralph Waldo Emerson and of other thinkers associated with Transcendentalism, and he pondered many of the same issues with which they grappled.

His own spiritual and intellectual journey influenced Henry James, Sr. in rejecting rote learning and unevaluated acceptance of beliefs as part of the educational process. He preferred to focus on the inner development of his children through observation and experience and to expose them to various forms of cultural expression in both America and Europe. He sent them to private schools, and engaged tutors for them.

Rich though their instruction was, it was also erratic. The younger boys suffered more from the frequent change that characterized it than did the older two. Moreover, their father favored the needs and desires of William and Henry over those of Wilkie and Bob. This, along with the inconsistency of their education, a family tendency toward emotional instability, and the availability of family money to insulate them from the consequences of their decisions, ultimately hindered Wilkie and Bob in finding direction. William James made his mark on American thought as a philosopher and psychologist, Henry, Jr. on literature as an observant and prolific author. But Wilkie and Bob were far less successful in fulfilling their potential.

Between 1858 and 1860, the Jameses traveled abroad specifically to expand the horizons of the children. By the summer of 1860, they were back in America. Henry, Sr. decided to send Wilkie and Bob to Frank Sanborn's private school in Concord, which had been established with Emerson's encouragement and opened in 1855. It must have been a shock for two boys fresh from the capitals of Europe to be deposited in Concord. Even their father understood this. After dropping them off, he wrote tellingly in a letter, "I buried two of my children yesterday—at Concord, Mass."

Sanborn's coeducational school was on Sudbury Road. Its progressive curriculum appealed to the boys' father. There were frequent excursions (for swimming, picnics, skating, horseback riding, and camping), dances, involvement in amateur theatricals with the Alcott girls, and considerable personal freedom. The faculty featured local talent—Henry David Thoreau, for example, who lectured and took the students for walks, and Elizabeth Ripley, who taught German. Sanborn's pupils included Edith, Ellen, and Edward Waldo Emerson, Julian Hawthorne, Sam Hoar (son of Ebenezer Rockwood Hoar), the Mann boys, and two daughters of Captain John Brown, on whose behalf the abolitionist Sanborn had raised money. Wilkie and Bob were popular with their classmates. But after the academic year 1860–1861, neither wanted to return. Wilkie was persuaded to do so, but Bob flatly refused.

The Civil War provided an unaccustomed sense of purpose for the two younger James boys. It was an opportunity for them to act upon their commitment to the abolition of slavery and at the same time to break free from their father's influence. Wilkie enlisted in 1862, after his second year at Sanborn's school, Bob in 1863. Both served in black regiments—Wilkie in Colonel Robert Gould Shaw's Massachusetts Fifty-fourth, Bob in the Massachusetts Fifty-fifth. Civil War service turned out to be the high point in the life of each.

After the war, backed by family money, the two went to Florida to run a cotton plantation with free black labor. They started out optimistically, but neither was a farmer or a businessman. The venture ultimately failed. Bob left Florida in 1867, Wilkie in 1871.

Bob had early shown artistic talent, but at this point his family encouraged him to think along more practical lines. He moved to Milwaukee, where, with the assistance of John Murray Forbes (father-in-law of Emerson's daughter Edith), he found work as a railroad clerk. He married Mary Holton in 1872. Unhappy in his position, he moved from place to place through a succession of other jobs. He became a heavy drinker, experienced mood swings and declining health. His personal problems affected his marriage. In 1871, after disentangling himself from the Florida fiasco, Wilkie, too, moved to Milwaukee. Like Bob, he was unhappy and unfulfilled there. He died in 1883.

In the early 1880s, Bob traveled east and studied art. Finally, in 1885, he moved permanently from Milwaukee to Concord with his wife and two children, Edward Holton (born in 1873) and Mary. Although he never achieved prominence as an artist, Robertson James found some measure of stability in Concord. He lived here from 1885 until his death, absent only for treatment of his alcoholism. He painted and wrote. In Concord directories for 1886 and 1892, his occupation is listed as "artist." He owned several properties and lived in various locations (on Main Street, on Nashawtuc Hill, and finally on Lexington Road), sometimes separately from his wife. After purchasing a house on Lexington Road, he built a studio on the property and lived in it. He died in 1910 and was buried in Sleepy Hollow.

After Bob's widow Mary died in 1922, her son Edward took possession of the Lexington Road house. Ned had graduated in 1896 from Harvard, where he was influenced by Emerson's writings. He had studied law at the University of Wisconsin, later practiced in Seattle. He was an author, lecturer, and an untiring political activist. Although he was regarded by many as a subversive, an anarchist, and a communist, he nevertheless considered himself deeply patriotic. He was particularly concerned with legal rights, civil liberties, equality for minorities, and world peace. In retrospect, the extreme positions that he took on various issues make it difficult to decide whether he was fundamentally liberal or conservative.

Edward James took on politics at both the national and the international level. In 1910, he helped overthrow King Manuel of Portugal. Before America's entrance into World War I, he was imprisoned in Germany for criticizing the Kaiser's government. In 1927, he championed Sacco and Vanzetti. Later, he established the Yankee Freemen Movement, and in 1943 published as its manifesto *I Am a Yankee*. Among the demands outlined by James in this booklet were a "Re-Declaration of Independence," "Re-establishment of the Monroe Doctrine and of George Washington's foreign policy," and safeguarding of the constitutional right of citizens to bear arms. James was charged with criminal libel in 1942 and jailed in Concord for distributing a handbill in which he called President Roosevelt and his administration "wreckers of the Republic" and "blood-stained assassins of our soldiers and sailors." The case was eventually dismissed. A prolific writer for newspaper publication, he also authored several books—*The Trial Before Pilate*; *Crossroads in Europe*; *I Tell Everything*; and *Jesus for Jews*.

Soon after he and his wife (Louisa Cushing James) moved into the Lexington Road house, Edward James replaced the studio his father had built with another of his own. (The couple also maintained a Boston address.) He repeated family history by living in it while his wife remained in the house. James diverted the Mill Brook into his basement to form a pond, where—as local historian Marian Miller reported in a 1978 biographical sketch—he kept a frog and a muskrat. He had a coffin in his bedroom, played the violin miserably but enthusiastically, and wandered about Concord with his instrument strapped to his back. Edward Holton James died in 1954 and was buried in the family plot in Sleepy Hollow.

It says something about Concord that Robertson James and his son felt sufficiently comfortable here to remain for much of their lives. Their experience highlights a local inclination to respect individuality, even when it is not fully in line with community values—a "live and let live" ethos. Bob and Ned James undoubtedly scandalized some of the people of Concord. Nevertheless, they paid a compliment to the town's tolerance in choosing to live and to exercise their personal freedoms here.

Robertson James painting the old Minot House, which formerly stood on Lexington Road.

*From an Alfred Munroe glass plate negative.*

## William Henry Hunt, from Punkatasset to Paris

William Henry Hunt, a seventh-generation Concordian, was born in 1839. At his death in 1926, he left twenty-five thousand dollars to the town "for the purpose of promoting the culture of school children by the erection of a gymnasium or otherwise." In 1933, a committee was appointed to study the building of a gymnasium, and two years later recommended that the Hunt legacy be combined with federal Public Works Administration funding to build the structure that Hunt had envisioned. The William Henry Hunt Memorial Gymnasium on Stow Street was ceremonially presented to the Concord School Committee on October 9, 1936. Turned over to the town by the School Department in the 1970s, extensively renovated in 1986 to serve as a community recreational center, the Hunt Gym still benefits Concord residents and municipal employees. The private story that led up to the establishment of this public facility is told in the manuscript reminiscences that Hunt prepared shortly before his death in 1926 for Allen French (his Social Circle biographer) and in other related sources. Hunt's life followed anything but a predictable path. Through native intelligence and some major good luck, William Henry Hunt surmounted early circumstances that might easily have extinguished his spirit, and became a pillar of the Concord community.

William Hunt—seventeenth-century ancestor of William Henry Hunt—bought land at Punkatasset Hill from Concord founder and first minister Peter Bulkeley. Generations of Hunts lived there and farmed the rocky soil over the centuries. Concord's first William Hunt and his sons Nehemiah and Isaac built a farmhouse that stood on the property, on what is now Monument Street, for more than two hundred years. According to Hunt family tradition, on April 19, 1775, food was provided for colonial troops at the Hunt farmhouse. In the early nineteenth century, a second, larger house, contiguous to the original, was added. William Henry Hunt's uncle Nehemiah and father Daniel inherited the ancestral property. After several years of unsuccessful farm management, Nehemiah sold his portion to Daniel, who managed it until William Henry took it over in the 1860s.

In 1825, Daniel Hunt married Clarissa Flint Cutter, a widow with a young daughter. Between 1826 and 1843, they had ten children. William Henry was the youngest of their four sons (one of whom died in infancy), and the second youngest child.

In his reminiscences, William Henry Hunt described his father Daniel as sober and hard-working, but endowed with neither the capital nor the temperament necessary to adapt to changing methods of farming and of marketing produce. The intertwining of his family's history with the town's invested Daniel Hunt with respectability, but he and his family lived in straitened circumstances. He had his hands full running his farm and providing for his large brood. Although not among Concord's poorer residents, he nevertheless had difficulty making ends meet. He had many children to feed, clothe, and educate and, because of the size of his family, insufficient resources to improve upon outdated methods of farm management. Moreover, he did not have enough sons to ease the burden of farm work and to help generate surplus for market. He was locked into a hard way of life, characterized by intense labor and little leisure to develop the higher sensibilities. He provided the basics—food for his wife to put on the table and the materials for her to make the family's clothing. The children got the rudiments of education in Concord's district school system. What little money was left over was used to send some of them to private academies and one to normal (teachers' training) school. But William Henry received his entire, meager formal education in District School No. 7. Reflecting on his childhood at the end of his life, he wrote starkly in a letter to Allen French, "At school I learned nothing."

Like his siblings, William Henry was intelligent and thoughtful. He learned to read and to think despite his limiting childhood environment. His intellectual horizons widened as he grew older. Allen French wrote in his Social Circle memoir that "in the end he was a cultured man." The Hunt girls, however, felt oppressed and thwarted by the constraints upon their opportunities. Their father's desire to educate his children to the best of his ability did not alter the fact that his daughters' prospects for the future were limited to marriage, teaching school, domestic positions, work in the mills in nearby Lowell or Lawrence, or spinsterhood within the family circle. In July of 1845, William Henry's sister Martha—a Concord district school teacher—succumbed to despair over her situation and drowned herself in the Concord River. (Author Nathaniel Hawthorne, who lived at the Old Manse on Monument Street from 1842 to 1845, recorded his vivid impressions of the search for her body in a lengthy journal entry, and drew on this account in describing the search for Zenobia's body in his *Blithedale Romance*, published in 1852). A second Hunt daughter later drowned herself near the spot where Martha had died, and a third sister subsequently drowned accidentally, according to local records.

Difficult though life was for Daniel Hunt and his family, and removed though their home was from the town center, they were nevertheless connected to the community in various ways. William Henry sold berries and delivered butter in the village, and did errands for his father as required. The family attended church at the First Parish. People in the neighborhood of Punkatasset made a point of visiting one another for conversation and companionship, particularly during the winter months. As an old man, William Henry Hunt fondly recalled the friendly gatherings around the fire in his home: "Of all the impressions received by my slowly unfolding mind in my childhood surroundings, there are none more firmly imprinted, clearly cut, or more free from all sorrowful suggestions." Moreover, Clarissa Cutter—Clarissa Hunt's daughter by her first marriage, and William Henry's half-sister—lived in and helped to manage the Main Street household of Ebenezer Rockwood and Caroline Brooks Hoar.

Although Daniel Hunt could not give his children material advantages, he possessed a respect for basic human rights that deeply impressed and remained with his son. William Henry never forgot his father's strong antislavery position and his willingness to express it. His recollections of his father's abolitionism highlight the underdocumented fact that antislavery sentiment in Concord cut across economic and class lines.

The inadequacy of his family's resources to nourish intellect and soul instilled in William Henry Hunt a powerful sense of the importance of education. He made self-culture a lifelong habit. Fond of solitude, as a child he roamed the fields and woods and, under the influence of Monument Street neighbor Minot Pratt, collected plant specimens—an early expression of interest in natural science. Later, he applied himself to subjects of practical use in farming. He was a member of the Middlesex Agricultural Society and, more significantly, of the Concord Farmers' Club, which provided a forum for discussion of topics of practical value and a stimulus to experimentation with crops, equipment, and techniques. Later, improved financial circumstances provided him with increased scope for self-culture and a rich inner life. He had a personal library, read extensively, traveled in Europe (he loved Switzerland and Paris), and learned what he could from his more cultivated associates. Allen French wrote that he also attended sessions of Bronson Alcott's Concord School of Philosophy in the 1880s. Hunt expressed his belief in the importance of education through repeated service on Concord's School Committee, through his bequest to build a gymnasium for the children of the town, and in a legacy to the Concord Free Public Library for the purchase of scientific books.

William Henry Hunt's successful transformation into a progressive farmer was made possible by his marriage to a somewhat older woman of means—a life-changing opportunity which he had the good sense to seize. He fell in love with, and, in 1859—at the age of twenty—married Elizabeth Baker, a cultured woman some ten years his senior, who brought a son of about eight to the union. Their marriage not only provided affection and emotional support but also significantly improved his financial situation. Elizabeth Baker Hunt's inheritance from her family eventually allowed her husband to put money into the ancestral Hunt farm and to raise himself out of the confining circumstances of his childhood into prosperity. After serving in the Civil War, Hunt settled down to running the old farm.

William Henry Hunt in his prime.

*From an Alfred Munroe glass plate negative.*

Having observed his father's struggles, he understood in maturity that only those farmers willing to invest in their farms and to adapt to changing market demands could thrive. Although he struggled with a variety of problems, he was young, a hard worker, and unencumbered by the large number of dependents his father had had to support. Able to hire help and to make necessary purchases and improvements, he did what his father had not attempted—he put the family farm on a scientific basis, successfully responded to the growing demand for delicate produce that could be transported by railroad to bigger markets beyond Concord, and tapped into the dairy market as well.

As Hunt established himself as a successful farmer, he increasingly took part in local government and organizations, and became a mainstay of the community. In addition to serving on the School Committee many times, he was an assessor, a member of the 1875 Committee of Arrangements for the centennial celebration of the Concord Fight, a selectman, an overseer of the poor, and a road commissioner. He was elected a member of the Social Circle in Concord in 1882, and was a founding member of the Concord Antiquarian Society in 1886. As a Civil War veteran, he commanded the Old Concord Post (No. 180) of the Grand Army of the Republic. He built a new house across the road from the family farmhouse, and later sold the property where the old place stood. (It was subsequently torn down.) In 1885, he and his wife represented the old blood of Concord in helping to organize a Hunt family reunion in the town. They opened the ancestral farmhouse to visitors from far and near, all descendants of the original William Hunt.

Following his wife's death in 1903, William Henry Hunt—the last member of his family to farm the fields by Punkatasset—sold his home, and subsequently divided his time between lodgings in Concord and relatives in Belmont (Massachusetts) and California. Although deaf, he retained his faculties, his sense of humor, and his dignity until the end of his life. In 1926, he was buried with military honors in Sleepy Hollow.

The Hunt Gym—conceived to foster the balanced development of the next generation—was a carefully considered gift made in response to difficult life-lessons learned early by this sensitive man. Although Daniel Hunt's relation to a first settler of Concord assured him and his family of community respect at a time when ancestry still mattered a good deal, it did nothing to advance his children's situation in life.

His youngest son's success was largely the result of a determined ability to make the most of circumstances and opportunities. Mindful that Concord honored his origins, provided latitude for his development, and embraced him as his upward financial mobility increasingly allowed him to take an active role in community life, he channeled his energy and resources into the town. Local people may no longer know much about the man responsible for the Hunt Recreation Center and for the purchase of valuable additions to the public library collection, but his name, at least, lingers on in community memory as that of a solid Concordian.

## Theodore Baker

Elizabeth Baker, who married farmer William Henry Hunt in 1859, was born in Philadelphia in 1830 to Thomas and Anne Izard McEuen (McEwen). Her son Theodore, born in 1851 in New York, was old enough to be taken for his young stepfather's brother rather than his stepson. Hunt and Baker no doubt became acquainted because they lived near one another on Punkatasset Hill. Elizabeth Baker lived in a building that had been used as a school by Marianne Ripley, sister of Brook Farm founder George Ripley. The structure (which no longer stands) served as the Hunts' home after their marriage, until the early 1880s, when they built a spacious new house.

In providing information to Allen French for his Social Circle memoir of William Henry Hunt, Mary Jacobs (Hunt's niece) noted that the groom's family was not in favor of the marriage. She wrote, "My Uncle's family were much distressed at first, at the thought of his marriage—(being a boy of twenty), to an older woman, mother of a son six or seven years old;—but he says, then, although he was under age, they knew he must 'have his own way.'" The age difference between Hunt and Baker, the responsibilities presented by her bringing a child to the marriage, and perhaps even the fact that she had come to Concord from elsewhere—that she was an outsider—might well have raised objections. Even decades later, Allen French described the relationship as a "strange romance."

Characteristically reticent about personal matters, William Henry Hunt did not comment in his reminiscences or his communications with Allen French about his marriage. The details of how and why Elizabeth Baker came to Concord are undiscovered. However, there are hints of why she—in Mary Jacobs's estimation "a very cultivated woman with an unusual education for those days"—would have been drawn to marry a younger man of little education, no means, and no experience of the world.

In 1922, artist Edward Emerson Simmons—a son of the Reverend George Frederick Simmons and Mary Emerson Ripley Simmons, and a great-grandson of Ezra Ripley—published his autobiography *From Seven to Seventy: Memories of a Painter and a Yankee*, the first chapter of which dealt with his early life in Concord. Discussing his mother's independence, Simmons—who grew up on Monument Street, by and in the Old Manse—wrote: "A woman had come to Concord, with no husband, and given birth to a child. This, for New England at that time, was a terrible scandal. The boy was my age [Simmons was born in 1852]. All the other boys whispered behind his back as if he had been in jail, although by this time his mother was properly married to a young farmer up on Barret's Hill [Punkatasset]. No one ever spoke to her in church or bowed. My mother, very quietly, every summer, put on her best clothes and walked the mile or more up the hill to call."

Although Elizabeth Baker's son was not born in Concord, Simmons's chronology and most of the circumstances in his account strongly suggest that he referred to Mrs. Hunt in this passage. While Simmons is not an especially reliable source, there is probably some kernel of truth in his assessment of Elizabeth Baker's social standing. Whether or not she was widowed rather than divorced or simply unmarried (although Allen French used the word "widow" in his Social Circle memoir, it is absent from the biographical information that Mary Jacobs provided to him), and whether or not her son was—as Simmons insinuated—illegitimate, the respectability of an out-of-town woman of mysterious origins living and raising a child on her own would have concerned many mid-nineteenth-century New Englanders. In marrying William Henry Hunt, Elizabeth Baker probably sought acceptance for herself and her son.

Elizabeth Hunt not only provided material support to her husband but also exerted a positive influence on his intellectual and aesthetic development. Theirs was an unconventional marriage, but apparently one that served both their needs. As William Henry Hunt's place in the community grew, so did his wife's. She was a member of the Concord Female Charitable Society, played the organ at the First Parish, became a member of the Trinitarian Congregational Church in 1887, and served as a judge of fancy articles and needlework at the Middlesex Agricultural Society Cattle Show.

In 1861, the couple had a son named William, who died a few days after birth. They raised Theodore, who used the last name Hunt while in his stepfather's household. Did the young people of Concord treat Theodore more respectfully after his mother's marriage became an accepted local fact? It is not known, and possibly unknowable. But the fact that he grew up, left Concord, and achieved considerable success without leaving an impress on local memory indicates that whatever bonds to community he formed while living in the town were easily loosened once he left to pursue his own life.

There is very limited local documentation of Theodore Hunt's life in Concord while growing up. Among the records of music-related expenses in the records of the First Parish, there are a number of receipts for payments made to his mother for playing the organ in the church between 1867 and 1869. In addition, there is a single receipt, dating from September of 1871, for payment to Theodore Hunt for performing the same service. This slip of paper provides the thin thread of evidence linking Theodore Hunt of Concord to the well-known music scholar and lexicographer Theodore Baker, author of a dictionary of musical terms (published in 1895) and of a biographical dictionary of music (1900) that is still, in much expanded and revised form, a standard resource today.

Theodore Baker is written up in a number of reference works about music and music history, which give his year of birth as 1851—the same year in which Elizabeth Baker Hunt's son was born. Although the compilers of these sources seem to have had access to little information about Baker's early background, or perhaps little inclination to go into it in depth, several of them note that he played the organ in Concord, Massachusetts, for a time.

Baker trained early for business but abandoned it for music. He studied in Germany in the 1870s, wrote a dissertation on the music of the Seneca tribe in New York (described as "the first serious work on American Indian music"), and received his doctoral degree at Leipzig in 1882. He came back to America in 1890 or 1891, and in 1892 became literary editor and translator for the music publisher Schirmer, in which capacity he translated many books, librettos, and articles from German into English. He returned to Germany in 1926—the year the long-widowed William Henry Hunt passed away—and died in Dresden in 1934. Baker is remembered not only for his scholarly compilations but also for his translation into English of the lyrics to the Thanksgiving hymn that begins "We gather together to ask the Lord's blessing"—a fact that calls to mind the New England veneration of Thanksgiving expressed in William Henry Hunt's reminiscences.

Did Theodore Baker's mother and stepfather support him in his decision to devote himself to music instead of business? Did he maintain close relations with them in adulthood? Did he remember Concord at all warmly? It is difficult to say, because he simply dropped off the local radar screen once he moved on. But it is clear that the foundation for his important contributions was built during his formative years, and that although Concord lost track of him as a local product, he developed the aptitude that led to his calling while living in the town.

What a contrast there is between Concord's forgetfulness of Baker and its pride in composer and music educator Thomas Whitney Surette, who served as organist for the First Parish between 1881 and 1892. But then, Surette was born in Concord, settled here in maturity, felt that his talents were locally appreciated, and chose to showcase and promote the town in his work. Baker was born elsewhere, at least initially seems to have lived here under a cloud that alienated him from the community, moved away, devoted his professional energies entirely to subjects and audiences other than Concord, and, after leaving, neglected to cultivate ties with the place beyond whatever family obligations he may have continued to fulfill. Even though he was an intimate household member of a man for whom Concord life was vitally important, Theodore Baker has remained an outsider.

CHAPTER V

# HIGHER CONCERNS

Concord today enfolds within its definition of spirituality much that extends beyond traditional worship. The idea that the town is by its very topography particularly receptive to emanations of spirit is commonplace. Those sensitive to expressions of the mystical often focus on the confluence of the Sudbury and Assabet Rivers at Egg Rock—where the Concord River begins and the earlier Native American presence is still felt—as a place of elemental significance. Some area residents gather at the confluence each June and December to celebrate the seasonal waxing and waning of light with drum and song. Musketaquid, the Indian name for Concord, evoking both river and surrounding grassy ground, is applied to a variety of activities affirming a sense of primal connectedness to the earth. One line of historical interpretation uses the rivers as a starting point in answering the question of why Concord nurtured Revolutionary independence in the eighteenth century, and radical thought and zeal for reform in the nineteenth.

Many residents and visitors alike see Concord as sacred ground because it was home to Emerson and Thoreau—spokesmen *par excellence* for the interrelatedness of God, man, and nature and for the divinity within every individual, and champions of spirit against the burgeoning materialism of their time. The example of such predecessors heightens present-day local awareness of the innate potential for spiritual development, and also imposes a particular sense of the responsibility to nurture this capacity. This legacy has influenced the course both of organized worship and of alternative expressions of spirituality here.

In 2000, an organization called Riverbend Landing published *A Resource Guide for the Spirit: Concord/Carlisle Massachusetts*, which was offered to the community as a record of "the activities, endeavors, places, and sources many recognize as possibilities for connection to Spirit." Illustrated with sketches of the confluence at

Egg Rock, this spiral-bound volume includes listings not only for area churches and synagogue, but also for an astonishing variety of organizations, institutions, and individuals devoted to one degree or another to nurturing mind, body, and soul—the Baha'i faith; a contemplative prayer group; spiritual healers; acupuncture specialists, and practitioners of alternative medicine and massage therapy; teachers of yoga, meditation, Reiki, Feng Shui, and T'ai Chi; promoters of wellness, nutrition, and fitness; clairvoyants; social service, human rights, and peace organizations; entities devoted to art, music, dance, writing, and theater; museums, historic houses, and libraries; environmental, land conservation, and animal rescue groups; adult education and enrichment opportunities; career counselors; and more. The range of entries gathered under the broad heading of spirit suggests that (like Emerson, Thoreau, and their Transcendental contemporaries) many Concordians now approach formal religion as only one avenue to connection with God and with the natural world, and to the elevation of spirit over matter.

Observations by area residents on the spiritual condition of Concord also dot the pages of this compilation. These assessments run the gamut from assertions of exceptional spirituality of place, to more qualified judgments, to one rather dark statement that the town is money-oriented and without soul. This mixed response reveals an undercurrent of tension between the desire for the rich inner life that many Concordians today accept as an attainable ideal and the suspicion that present-day materialism complicates its achievement. Some are tempted to look to the circumstances of times past as more conducive than modern life to idealism and spiritual development. Nevertheless, Concordians from Peter Bulkeley on have been conscious of the uneasy coexistence here of spirituality and idealism on the one hand, and materialism on the other.

In his 1835 Concord address, Ralph Waldo Emerson lingered over the Reverend Bulkeley's desire for religious freedom as a chief cause behind Concord's founding. He presented Bulkeley—parish minister in Bedfordshire, England, and the first in the line of Concord clergymen from whom Emerson himself descended—as a nonconformist induced by persecution in his native land "to overcome that natural repugnance to emigration which holds the serious and moderate of every nation to their own soil." He quoted from Bulkeley's *Gospel-Covenant* to suggest that an extraordinary religious spirit provided the sustaining strength necessary to endure the danger and deprivation inherent in carving a town out of the wilderness. Concord's English settlers, Emerson proclaimed, "conspired with their teacher"—Bulkeley—and found in their religion "sweetness and peace amidst toil and tears." This filiopietistic slant on Concord's beginnings as a town suited the celebratory occasion for which Emerson wrote these words. But elsewhere, he expressed awareness that seventeenth-century Concordians were moved at least as much by material as by spiritual concerns.

In the poem "Hamatreya" (first published some eleven years after the bicentennial of Concord's incorporation), Emerson treated Concord's settlers entirely as material men, omitting to tell his readers anything of them as religious, emotional, or intellectual men. The founders took satisfaction in their ownership of the trees and hills, and believed that the land would belong to them and to their descendants forever. In pointing out that these men now lie "Asleep beneath their grounds," Emerson suggested that acquisition as a value is temporal and illusory. In counterpoint to the spiritual emphasis in the 1835 address, the focus on materialism in "Hamatreya" underscored Emerson's divided feelings about his hometown—at its founding and in his own time—and about human nature in general.

Concord's past yields many examples of the impetus toward ideals higher than the material concerns of the moment. The life and background of Mary Merrick Brooks, a woman who made the abolition of slavery her personal crusade, shows that the impulse to right injustice against human dignity is sometimes driven by interaction between personal history and a purer idealism. The story of spiritualism in Concord and elsewhere in the 1850s highlights the popularity of one alternative means of making the leap from material to spiritual. The establishment of Sleepy Hollow Cemetery in 1855 constitutes a tangible and successful local attempt to embody the ideal in the material. And, finally, the community's kindness in 1887 to one Concord School of Philosophy participant demonstrates the basic respect that the town has extended to spiritual pilgrims and seekers of the ideal even when failing to share full-blown enthusiasm for their pursuits. Reconciling idealism, spirituality, and materialism is far from a local concern, but it is one with which Concordians at large—not only major historical figures like Puritan Peter Bulkeley, evangelical minister Daniel Bliss, and Transcendentalists Emerson, Thoreau, and Alcott—have grappled repeatedly.

## Slaveholding and Abolition in One Concord Family

Mary Merrick Brooks—daughter of Concord storekeeper Tilly Merrick and wife of lawyer Nathan Brooks—was recognized during her life and has been celebrated since her death in 1868 as the strong and dedicated leader of the radical Concord Ladies' Antislavery Society. A founding member in 1837 and a longtime officer of the Society, a respected associate of abolitionists William Lloyd Garrison and Wendell Phillips, and a member of the Middlesex County Antislavery Society as well, Mrs. Brooks was characterized by Harriet Robinson in *Warrington Pen-Portraits* (1877) as the "chief organizer and inspirer" of antislavery activism in Concord.

Born in 1801 to Tilly and Sally (Minot) Merrick, Mary Merrick developed into "the most beautiful young lady in town" in the opinion of Edward Jarvis, who so described her in a manuscript annotation in his personal copy of Shattuck's *History of the Town of Concord*. In 1823, she married Nathan Brooks, a widower with a young daughter, Caroline (later Mrs. Ebenezer Rockwood Hoar). Nathan and Mary Brooks had two sons, George Merrick (eventually a lawyer and a judge) and Charles Augustus (who died before he was a year old). The Brooks family lived in the house that then stood at the intersection of Main Street and Sudbury Road, later the site of the Concord Free Public Library.

During the nineteenth century, community organizations provided women with an outlet beyond family and home for the expression of intellect, organizational ability, and social conscience. From 1814, many women of the town belonged to the Concord Female Charitable Society, which provided local aid. From the 1830s, the antislavery movement offered opportunity for women to bring social reality in line with the democratic and religious ideal of the brotherhood of all men by subverting the sanctioned treatment of human beings as material property, and to achieve in the process an enhanced sense of purpose, validation, and companionship. During the Civil War, Concord ladies threw their energies into the important work of the Soldiers' Aid Society. Later in the century, the Women's Parish Association of the First Parish was formed so that women might play a more active role in aspects of church management.

As Harriet Robinson recorded, Mary Merrick Brooks's comrades in the Ladies' Antislavery Society included Cynthia, Helen, and Sophia Thoreau (mother and sisters of Henry David Thoreau), Maria King Prescott (Mrs. Timothy Prescott), Maria Pratt (Mrs.

Minot Pratt), Lidian and Ellen Emerson (wife and daughter of Ralph Waldo Emerson), Ann Bigelow (Mrs. Francis E. Bigelow), Abigail May Alcott (Mrs. Bronson Alcott), Caroline Brooks Hoar (Mrs. E.R. Hoar, stepdaughter of Mary Merrick Brooks), Mary Rice, and sisters Louisa and Anna Whiting. These women organized fairs and socials to raise funds for their cause. (Mary Brooks was famous for her "Brooks Cake," which was sold at such events to provide Garrison and others with the money necessary to transform moral outrage into political action.) They arranged for inspiring lecturers. For example, Ralph Waldo Emerson delivered a stirring address in the courthouse on Monument Square on August 1, 1844, on the anniversary of emancipation in the British West Indies, at the request of Mrs. Brooks. After passage of the Compromise of 1850 and the detested Fugitive Slave Law, some—including Mary Brooks—offered runaway slaves en route to freedom safe haven in their homes through the network known as the Underground Railroad.

The Brooks House at the intersection of Main Street and Sudbury Road, 1860s, prior to its move to Hubbard Street and the construction of the Concord Free Public Library on the site.

*From an early photographic print.*

Mary Merrick Brooks was undoubtedly motivated in her efforts by a desire to bring about meaningful change. But another, more personal factor likely also contributed to the fervor she brought to the antislavery cause. Decades before she turned her attention to abolition, her father was a plantation and slave owner in South Carolina—a fact that must have been ever on his daughter's mind as she labored on behalf of the enslaved.

Tilly Merrick was born in Concord in 1755. After his father's death in 1768, his mother married widower Duncan Ingraham, a sea captain and merchant involved in the slave trade, a slaveholder, a British sympathizer during the Revolution, and a man given to the display of his money and taste. Since Concord was a community in which slave ownership was not widespread, Ingraham's slaves drew attention to the man's wealth and ostentation. Young Merrick graduated from Harvard in 1773. Although he was in Concord on April 19, 1775, he spent most of the Revolution abroad. His biography in the Second Series of *Memoirs of Members of the Social Circle in Concord* describes him as "connected with the embassy of John Adams to France and Holland, as an *attaché*." How formal that arrangement was remains unclear, as does the extent of the responsibilities it entailed. While abroad, he had sufficient free time to involve himself in international shipping in Amsterdam, in the firm of Sigourney, Ingraham & Co. (The Ingraham in the partnership was his stepfather's son.)

After the war ended, Tilly Merrick returned to America, to Charleston, South Carolina, where he became a partner in the shipping firm of Merrick & Course, as the abundant records generated by his business life document. He enjoyed considerable financial success for some time, and bought—as stated in his Social Circle memoir—"large plantations at Eighteen Mile Creek, with the usual accompaniment of horses, hogs, negroes, and other [chattel]." Merrick clearly had no qualms about fitting into the Southern economy and way of life. But his prosperity did not last. Having lost most of what he had acquired in South Carolina, he returned to Concord in 1798, married Sally Minot, settled on Merrick family property along the south side of Main Street and Sudbury Road, and opened a general store. After the relative glamour and excitement of shipping in Amsterdam and Charleston, he had difficulty adjusting to storekeeping in what was—with a population of fewer than seventeen hundred people in 1800—a small New England town. He devoted himself halfheartedly to managing his store and as a consequence never did very well. He sold the business to Phineas Howe in the early 1820s. Tilly Merrick died in 1836, the year before his daughter and other Concord women banded together to fight slavery.

In light of her father's earlier complicity in the institution that she worked to eradicate, Mary Merrick Brooks's leadership of the Concord Ladies' Antislavery Society takes on considerable psychological complexity. Significantly, in a 1909 biographical lecture on Caroline Brooks Hoar, Bessie Keyes Hudson wrote: "Mrs. Brooks' father, Mr. Merrick, was a slave-owner, and at first Mrs. Brooks' sympathies were on that side. She is said to have gone to an anti-slavery meeting and to have been converted on the spot." The suggestion that Mary Merrick Brooks was a convert to the antislavery cause is intriguing. An experience of personal transformation would go far toward explaining the total commitment and boldness in action that made her a driving force behind the abolition movement in Concord.

## "Taps in the Wall, & Thumps in the Table-Drawer"

In 1848, sisters Margaret and Kate Fox of Hydesville, New York, reported hearing rappings in their bedroom, unexplained sounds that were interpreted as communications from the dead. The Foxes' story spread rapidly, sparking broad interest in spiritualism in this country and beyond in the 1850s. The two sisters became media celebrities and objects of public display. Others quickly established themselves as mediums, providing a conduit between this world and the next for a fee. Publications devoted to promoting spiritualism helped to popularize the phenomenon, which was eagerly embraced in small towns as well as in cities. Spiritualism in the 1850s took a variety of forms. Mediums presided over séances, encouraging the departed to manifest themselves through noises such as those the Foxes had heard, through music, through the spontaneous movement of furniture and other objects, as apparitions, or in writing (via the medium's hand). Mesmerism, or hypnotism, also provided access to the beyond.

In Concord, as elsewhere, opinion on spiritualism was divided. Some were enthusiastic, like Elizabeth Palmer Peabody—reformer, educator, frequent visitor to Concord from the late 1830s, and later a local resident. Peabody attended séances in Boston and believed that she had made contact with her deceased mentor, Dr. William Ellery Channing. Others—like Ralph Waldo Emerson, Henry David

Thoreau, and Ebenezer Rockwood Hoar—were skeptical, even con-temptuous. Scornful though Thoreau and Emerson may have been, their comments on the subject indicate that spiritualism had found a following in Concord by the early 1850s.

On March 5, 1852, Thoreau wrote of a Dr. Dillingham, who was interested in the "spiritual knockers" and had had them at his house. The reference is probably to physician Nathan H. Dillingham, who was included in the 1850 federal census for Concord. A few months later, on July 13, 1852, Thoreau complained in a letter to his sister Sophia that Concord was "just as idiotic as ever in relation to the spirits and their knockings." He went on to express disgust with the vision of eternal life held by his spiritualistic townsmen: "If I could be brought to believe in the things which they believe, I should make haste to get rid of my certificate of stock in this and the next world's enterprises, and buy a share in the first Immediate Annihilation Company that offered."

Emerson, too, wrote disparagingly. In a June/July 1852 journal entry, he mentioned a "Miss Bridge, a mantuamaker [dressmaker] in Concord," who had become a medium, charging "a pistareen a spasm, and nine dollars for a fit." "This," Emerson continued, "is the Rat-revelation, the Gospel that comes by taps in the wall, & thumps in the table-drawer." The probable object of Emerson's scorn in this passage was Louisia M. Bridge, a dressmaker, according to the 1860 federal census.

In his essay "Worship" (published in *The Conduct of Life*), Emer-son echoed the wording of his journal entry about Miss Bridge, writ-ing of "the squalor of Mesmerism, the deliration of rappings, the rat and mouse revelation, thumps in table-drawers, and black art." In a footnote to this passage in the 1904 Centenary Edition volume of *The Conduct of Life*, Emerson's son Edward elaborated on the mid-nine-teenth-century invasion of Concord by spiritualism, commenting that its "chief exponent" was a "Mr. M———," whom he described as "a humble maker of pocket-books in Concord." Through the family papers of nineteenth-century Concord lawyer Nathan Brooks, it is possible both to identify the mysterious Mr. M——— and to under-stand something of the reasons for his excursions into the spiritual world. The Brooks papers incorporate those of Augustus Merrick, Brooks's brother-in-law, and include a file of Merrick's communica-tions through mediums with his dead parents in the 1850s.

Augustus Merrick descended through his mother from the Minots, who came to Concord in the seventeenth century. He was the second son and last of four children of Concord storekeeper Tilly Merrick and Sally Minot Merrick. His sister was antislavery activist Mary Merrick Brooks. Augustus was born in Concord in 1810, never married, and died in 1871. He is described in the business papers he left behind, in Concord assessors' records, and in the federal census as a pocketbook maker. He produced porte-monnaies (money purses), needlebooks, and other leather items. From the mid-1830s through the 1840s, he lived away from Concord. Mail was sent to him at Boston and Cambridgeport addresses. By the late 1840s, he was back here. He appears in the Concord assessors' records continuously from 1849 through 1859, when he evidently left town again.

Despite his Concord heritage and family connections, Augustus Merrick was a ne'er-do-well. His financial papers for the late 1830s and the 1840s show mounting debt and money owed him but not paid. He declared bankruptcy in 1848, at about the time he came back to Concord. For several years after his return, he continued working as a pocketbook maker. Assessors' records show that he owned no real estate, but in the early 1850s had stock in trade, which disappears from his valuations from 1853 on.

Sally Minot Merrick died in 1816, Tilly Merrick in 1836. Prone to mismanaging money and worried about the state of his health, Augustus Merrick sorely needed parental advice and comfort after his return to Concord. In their absence, he engaged the services of mediums. Merrick's papers include messages from his dead parents and others, written in several manuscript hands, plus a printed business card for a Boston medium. The messages from his father and mother suggest that the mediums Merrick consulted were at least as adept at psychology as they were at parapsychology. They overflow with concern for his physical and mental well-being and with helpful counsel, including warnings against his use of tobacco—exactly the kind of support that Merrick's parents might have offered in person had they been alive.

In an age of increasing mechanization and materialism, Emerson and Thoreau celebrated the divine and constant. In its own way, spiritualism offered another means of coping with change and of bridging the gap between the material and the spiritual.

## H.W.S. Cleveland, Designer of Sleepy Hollow

Since its dedication on September 29, 1855, Sleepy Hollow Cemetery has been a source of pride for the town, the final resting place for many local residents, and—largely because of the constellation of nineteenth-century literary luminaries buried on Authors' Ridge—a tourist stop on the Concord itinerary. Laid out on land purchased from the estate of Deacon Reuben Brown, Sleepy Hollow was named, according to George Bradford Bartlett in his 1880 *Concord Guide Book*, for the natural "amphitheatre" that "had borne the name of Sleepy Hollow long before it was thought of as a place of burial." (Bartlett's amphitheatre was the larger of two deep hollows, or kettle holes, within the cemetery's bounds.) The choice of name may or may not also have reflected local familiarity with Washington Irving's "The Legend of Sleepy Hollow," published in 1820 in Irving's *Sketch Book*. Ralph Waldo Emerson remarked in his address at the dedication of the cemetery upon Sleepy Hollow's "seclusion from the village in its immediate neighborhood," which had long made the area "an easy retreat on a Sabbath day, or a summer twilight."

As Concord's Superintendent of Grounds during the planning and laying out of Sleepy Hollow, John Shepard Keyes—lawyer, judge (from 1874), and public official at the local, state, county, and national levels—was responsible for the maintenance and improvement of the town's cemeteries. Never a man to underplay his role in events, Keyes was inclined to take the lion's share of credit for bringing the cemetery into being. In his manuscript autobiography, he described laying out the cemetery, driving in the stakes for the lots, sparing "as many trees as possible from cutting," and arranging the dedication ceremonies. He wrote, "Thanks to me we have a 'Sleepy Hollow' cemetery. I am quite content to take my long sleep in [it] and [to take] for my only epitaph 'The Founder of This Cemetery.'"

In fact, at his death in 1910, Keyes was buried in a place of prominence on Authors' Ridge. The epitaph on the large stone he shares with Martha Lawrence Prescott Keyes, his wife of more than fifty years, proclaims the couple jointly "Founders of This Cemetery." Important though Keyes was in accomplishing the hands-on work necessary to make Sleepy Hollow a reality, however, he did not provide the creative vision that transformed the cemetery into the palpable expression of an aesthetic ideal. The plans for the cemetery were drawn by Horace William Shaler Cleveland and Robert Morris Copeland, partners in landscape design. The printed Concord town report for 1855–1856 shows that Cleveland and Copeland were paid seventy-five dollars for their work.

Copeland's connection with Sleepy Hollow seems to have left a deeper impression on local memory than did Cleveland's. Just twenty-five years after the cemetery opened, George Bartlett in his guidebook ascribed the plans for it entirely to Copeland, overlooking Cleveland altogether. That Copeland lived in Lexington, closer to Concord than did Cleveland, may have made him the better known of the two to people here. On January 10, 1855, Copeland delivered a lecture before the Concord Lyceum on "The Useful & The Beautiful" in art, architecture, landscape gardening, and cemetery design, as manuscript Lyceum records reveal. The public visibility that this lecture conferred made him the more likely professional contact with Concord decision-makers than his partner.

But Cleveland was without a doubt responsible in some measure for the design of Sleepy Hollow, and may well have exerted a greater influence than Copeland on the final result. Even John Shepard Keyes acknowledged in his autobiography that while he laid out Sleepy Hollow "almost alone and unaided," he did so "according to Cleveland's plan." Moreover, unlike Copeland, Cleveland enjoyed a long and continuously productive career as a landscape architect. He shaped public and private landscapes not only in New England but in the expanding American west, as well. In the process, he left behind many examples of public work that suggest just how much Concord's Sleepy Hollow owes to his transcendent—indeed, Transcendental—sense of the primacy of the natural landscape over design features.

H.W.S. Cleveland was born in 1814 in rural Lancaster, Massachusetts, to sea captain Richard Jeffry Cleveland and his wife Dorcas. In the late 1820s, the Clevelands moved to Cuba, where Richard held a diplomatic position. Having returned to America, young Horace found employment in the 1830s as a surveyor for railroad and real estate interests in Illinois and elsewhere out west. He came back to Massachusetts late in the decade. In the early 1840s, he bought a farm near Burlington, New Jersey, where he took up scientific farming and began writing for *The Horticulturist*, a periodical edited by renowned landscape gardener, architect, and horticulturist Andrew Jackson Downing.

Cleveland moved back to Massachusetts in 1854 (he lived first in Salem, then in Danvers), and entered into a partnership in landscape architecture with fellow scientific farmer R.M. Copeland. The design of Sleepy Hollow in the garden cemetery tradition of Cambridge's

Mount Auburn Cemetery (1831) was one of their first important commissions. In drawing up their plan, they avoided the imposition of a geometric grid of lots over the terrain, preferring instead to place lots on paths and drives that followed the natural outlines of the land, and respecting native trees and plants. The two went on to make recommendations for a Boston park system. In 1857, they entered the competition for the design of New York's Central Park, which Frederick Law Olmsted and his partner Calvert Vaux won. Cleveland and Copeland parted ways before the Civil War. Copeland served in the war and subsequently established his own landscape design practice, which thrived until his sudden death in 1872.

In 1869, Cleveland moved to Chicago, where he had a major impact on the developing park system and other public spaces. He formed a professional association with landscape architect William Merchant Richardson French, brother of Daniel Chester French and, for thirty-five years, director of the Art Institute of Chicago. Cleveland accepted commissions elsewhere in Illinois, and in Indiana, Michigan, Wisconsin, Iowa, Kansas, and Nebraska as well. He corresponded extensively with his professional peers (Olmsted among

Path in Sleepy Hollow Cemetery, late 19th century.
*From an Alfred Munroe glass plate negative.*

them) and wrote about landscape design. His influential *Landscape Architecture as Applied to the Wants of the West* was published in 1873. The public spaces of Minneapolis provided the final palette for Cleveland's talents. Having already worked on a number of commissions in that city, he moved there in 1886, and took on the design of the Minneapolis park system. He died in Hinsdale, Illinois, in 1900, and was buried in Minneapolis.

As landscape historian Daniel Nadenicek has suggested, Cleveland's personal brand of landscape design was informed by Emerson's organic approach to art and aesthetics. In his Sleepy Hollow dedication address, Emerson extolled the natural landscape as the proper focus of the landscape architect: "Modern taste has shown that there is no ornament, no architecture alone, so sumptuous as well disposed woods and waters, where art has been employed only to remove superfluities, and bring out the natural advantages." In his *A Few Words on the Arrangement of Rural Cemeteries* (1881), Cleveland echoed Emerson's emphasis on the natural landscape. He wrote critically of the tendency to lay out cemeteries "without the least regard to topographical features, or the opportunities for tasteful effects which the natural position may afford."

Along with maps and plans, printed tracts, and historical photographs, the landscape itself provides a form of documentation. One need only walk through the 1855 section of Sleepy Hollow to understand intuitively that its design was intended to foster tranquility and private contemplation. Cleveland's Transcendental sense of nature as a tonic for the soul and a catalyst for human sensibilities is clearly reflected in the curving paths and wooded rises of Concord's gem of a cemetery.

## Philosophy and Toadstools

Every summer between 1879 and 1887, Bronson Alcott's Concord School of Philosophy brought lecturers and audiences here to explore philosophy, celebrate literature, and rekindle the Transcendental idealism that earlier had inspired Emerson and his intellectual comrades to thought, writing, and reform activity. (The sole program for the 1888 final season was a memorial service on June 16th for Bronson Alcott, who died on March 4th of that year.) In his *Concord Historic, Literary and Picturesque* (an expansion of his 1880 *Concord Guide Book*), George Bradford Bartlett declared the aims of the school "to bring together a few of those persons who, in

America, have pursued, or desire to pursue the paths of speculative philosophy; to encourage these students and professors to communicate with each other what they have learned and meditated; and to illustrate by a constant reference to poetry and the higher literature." While those associated with the enterprise thrived in this heady atmosphere, local people were often amused and sometimes exasperated by the philosophical pilgrims who descended annually on Concord in search of higher truth and inexpensive lodgings.

The odd drama of one student's brush with dangerous materiality commanded the attention of school, town, and even the Boston press in the summer of 1887. *Boston Post* clippings (dated July 28 and 29, 1887) in a School of Philosophy scrapbook kept by William Torrey Harris—who with Frank Sanborn helped Bronson Alcott run the school, and who purchased the Orchard House in 1884—tell the story of Mrs. Abby Pratt of Woburn. An attendee of several summer sessions of the Concord School of Philosophy, Mrs. Pratt was eighty-three years old in 1887, and—not surprisingly—had some trouble getting around. Nevertheless, she was (according to one newspaper account) "zealous in her attendance and . . . seldom missed a lecture." Her earnest interest in (although perhaps not complete mastery over) the weighty topics to which the school was devoted is apparent in a letter she wrote to Harris on May 16, 1887.

The printed School of Philosophy program for 1887 indicates that the session that year ran from July 13th to July 31st and consisted of twelve morning lectures on Aristotle, ten evening lectures on dramatic poetry, and four additional brief papers on ontology. Mrs. Pratt usually listened to the morning lecture at the School of Philosophy's Hillside Chapel and then walked up the hill behind, where she read through the early afternoon.

On the morning of July 28th, Abby Pratt arranged to meet her sister—a Mrs. Thompson, also of Woburn, and also a student at the school—on the hill at one o'clock. Mrs. Thompson climbed to the appointed location at the prearranged time, but did not find Mrs. Pratt. After waiting for two hours, she searched to no avail for her sister. She then went to wait at the boardinghouse where Mrs. Pratt was staying and, later, to the evening lecture in the hope that the lady would show up there. Half an hour into the program, the anxious Mrs. Thompson took Frank Sanborn aside and told him that Mrs. Pratt was missing. Sanborn interrupted the proceedings to ask if anyone had seen Mrs. Pratt. When nobody offered information, William

Ordway Partridge picked up the program where he had left off. The reporter on the School of Philosophy for the *Boston Post* observed archly, "Old ladies may come, and old ladies may go, but philosophy goes on forever."

Although the *Boston Post* account may be more colorful than accurate in its details (William Torrey Harris wrote "Not correct account" next to one of the *Post* clippings in his scrapbook), it certainly makes a good story. Later in the evening, students of the school and locals together scoured the woods on the hill behind the chapel for signs of Mrs. Pratt. Around midnight, all but one—barge driver C.F. Watts—decided to suspend the search until daybreak. Watts's persistence was rewarded by the discovery of Mrs. Pratt lying stiff, cold, and unconscious on "Hawthorne's ledge," behind the Wayside. Revived by a mixture of brandy and milk and transported by carriage to her boardinghouse, Mrs. Pratt felt sufficiently well to talk about what had happened to her.

Mrs. Pratt and Mrs. Thompson had crossed wires about the exact spot on the hill where they were to meet. Consequently, Mrs. Pratt went without lunch for much longer than she had anticipated. She grew hungry, but had brought little to eat. Noticing what she thought was a "succulent mushroom" nearby, she picked and ate it. Unfortunately, what appeared to be a mushroom was, in fact, an inedible toadstool, and Mrs. Pratt lapsed into unconsciousness. Only her sturdy constitution and overall good health saved her from death. "Had the search for her been postponed until morning, she would then have been found a corpse," stated the report of her recovery in the July 29th issue of the *Boston Post*. The undaunted Mrs. Pratt planned to attend the scheduled School of Philosophy lecture the morning after her rescue, but was dissuaded by her sister from doing so. Her local physician (identified as Dr. George E. Titcomb in the brief paragraph in the *Concord Freeman* on the incident) urged her to rest in Concord for several days before returning home.

The incident of the poison toadstool undoubtedly did nothing to redeem Concord's resident and visiting philosophers in the eyes of skeptical observers. Idealism was an easy target in the materialistic 1880s. Alcott, Harris, Sanborn, and their associates and followers accepted the fact that not everyone was sympathetic to the life of the mind and spirit. They drew strength from the opportunity for companionship with others who shared their interests, in the process forming a distinct—if fluid—community within the larger community that hosted them. For their part, Concord residents, however disposed toward philosophical pursuit, offered these idealists the same common courtesy they extended to their next-door neighbors, thereby encouraging higher consciousness in their midst.

# ACKNOWLEDGMENTS

Faithful readers of my column "Historic Concord" (*The Concord Journal*, 2000–2005) have repeatedly asked when I would gather my separate articles for publication in book form. I thank them for the incentive to undertake *In History's Embrace*. Thanks, also, to former *Journal* editors Greg Turner and Maureen O'Connell for their commitment to the column.

*In History's Embrace* owes much to the support—moral and practical—of Barbara A. Powell, Director of the Concord Free Public Library, who encouraged weaving together these essays as a worthwhile expression of the library's central role in documenting and interpreting the social history of Concord. The Concord Free Public Library Corporation enabled the leap from manuscript to printed volume, and authorized the inclusion of the historic images that grace the pages of the finished product.

The library is fortunate to have a staunch friend in historian and Concord resident Doris Kearns Goodwin. On behalf of the entire library administration and staff, I thank her not only for contributing the foreword to *In History's Embrace*, but also for many other public expressions of support over the years.

Fellow Special Collections staff members Joyce T. Woodman (former Staff Assistant and my working comrade on and off for twenty-five years), Constance Manoli-Skocay (Staff Assistant since Joyce's retirement in 2005), and Robert C. Hall (Cataloger and Technical Services Associate) each made meaningful contributions. As installments of "Historic Concord" were published, Joyce was always happy to chat with me about the subject of a forthcoming column or to share her considerable insight into local source material. Conni read and responded to sections of an early version of the manuscript, reinforcing certain approaches as the book evolved. Bob prepared digital files from original photographs and assisted with the transmission of both text and images, counteracting my natural talent for electronic disaster. Others who work in the library—both staff and volunteers—expressed thoughtful interest in the book-in-progress.

Thanks to Reed Anthony, Jayne Gordon, Robert A. Gross, Sherry F. Litwack, Barbara Powell, Albrecht Saalfield, Joseph C. Wheeler, and David F. Wood for reading the manuscript with a critical eye, and offering comments. (I especially appreciate David Wood's bringing to my attention, and urging me to include, the fact that Henry David Thoreau was responsible for cutting Concord's community Christmas tree in 1853.) David Grayson Allen, Bob Gross, Megan Marshall, and Joel Myerson were generous in preparing jacket commentary. Library staff member Martha Proctor and volunteers Susan Hill Birge, Reed Anthony, and Gretchen W. O'Connor directed their keen powers of observation to proofreading.

Frederick S. Lyford and the staff of the Puritan Press/Hollis Publishing Company in Hollis, New Hampshire, have been most responsive to library requirements and concerns in the production of this book.

Finally, thanks to my husband Michael, daughters Monica, Ann, and Lillian, and grandbabies Cynthia and Jocelyn for their good-natured tolerance of my ongoing preoccupation with Concord.

LPW

# SOURCES
## (ESSAY BY ESSAY)

*For sources listed more than once, a full citation is given for the first reference, an abbreviated version for subsequent references.*

## PREFACE

Emerson, Ralph Waldo. *A Historical Discourse, Delivered Before the Citizens of Concord, 12th September, 1835. On the Second Centennial Anniversary of the Incorporation of the Town.* Concord: G.F. Bemis, 1835.

James, Henry. "Concord and Salem." *The American Scene.* New York: Penguin, 1994. 190–201.

Wheeler, Ruth Robinson. "Will Change Spoil Us?" *The Concord Journal* 3 Jan. 1946:1.

## I. IMAGE-SHAPING

### Lemuel Shattuck, Concord's First Historian:

Cassedy, James H. "Shattuck, Lemuel." *American National Biography.* 1999.

Emerson, Ralph Waldo. *A Historical Discourse.*

Hudson, Charles. "Memoir of Lemuel Shattuck." *Proceedings of the Massachusetts Historical Society* 18 (1880–81): 155–65.

Keyes, George. "Memoir of Lemuel Shattuck." *Memoirs of Members of the Social Circle in Concord.* Second Series. Concord: The Circle, 1888. 224–27.

Keyes, John Shepard. "Memoir of Daniel Shattuck." *Memoirs of Members of the Social Circle in Concord.* Second Series. 134–40.

Shattuck, Lemuel. *A History of the Town of Concord; Middlesex County, Massachusetts, from Its Earliest Settlement to 1832; and of the Adjoining Towns, Bedford, Acton, Lincoln, and Carlisle.* Boston: Russell, Odiorne; Concord: John Stacy, 1835.

Shattuck, Lemuel. "Lemuel Shattuck." *Memorials of the Descendants of William Shattuck, the Progenitor of the Families in America That Have Borne His Name.* Boston: Dutton and Wentworth for the Family, 1855. 302–12.

Thatcher, B.B. "Art. VI—History of Concord" (review of Shattuck's history, and of Emerson's bicentennial address). *The North American Review* 42 (1836): 448–67.

Willcox, Walter F. "Shattuck, Lemuel." *Dictionary of American Biography.* 1935.

**April 19, 1894: The First Official Patriots' Day:**

Hoar, Ebenezer Rockwood. *Speech at Concord, April 19, 1894.* Ms. Vault A45, Hoar Unit 3. William Munroe Special Collections, Concord Free Public Library, Concord, MA.

Love, W. DeLoss. *The Fast and Thanksgiving Days of New England.* Boston: Houghton Mifflin, 1895.

Massachusetts. *Commonwealth of Massachusetts. By His Excellency Frederic T. Greenhalge, Governor: A Proclamation. By an Act of the Legislature, duly approved, the Nineteenth Day of April Has Been Made a Legal Holiday* (broadside), 1894.

Shattuck, Lemuel. "Appendix. No. I. Historical View of the Evidence Relating to the Events of the 19th of April, 1775." *A History of the Town of Concord.* 333–51.

**Robert Frost a No-Show in 1925:**

Collection of Materials Relating to the 150th Anniversary Celebration in Concord, Mass., of the Battle of Concord, 1925–<1985>. Concord Pamphlet 71, Item 6. William Munroe Special Collections, CFPL.

Concord (MA). "Report of the Nineteenth of April Committee." *The Annual Report of the Officers of the Town of Concord Massachusetts from January 1, 1925, to December 31, 1925.* Concord: The Town, 1926. 48–49.

"Final Program for the Celebration of the 150th Anniversary of the Concord Fight. April 19th–20th—Concord Massachusetts." *Concord Enterprise* 15 Apr. 1925: 1.

Jarvis, Edward. "Second Centennial Celebration." *Traditions and Reminiscences of Concord, Massachusetts, 1779–1878.* Ed. Sarah Chapin. Amherst: U Massachusetts P, 1993. 33–39. (This edition of *Traditions and Reminiscences* includes Jarvis's annotations to his personal copy of Shattuck's Concord history.)

Katz, Sandra L. *Elinor Frost: A Poet's Wife.* Westfield, MA: Inst. for Massachusetts Studies, Westfield State Coll., 1988.

Nineteenth of April Committee for the Celebration in Concord, Mass., of the 150th Anniversary of the Battle of Concord. Records, 1924–26. Vault A15, Unit C4. William Munroe Special Collections, CFPL.

150th anniversary of the Battle of Concord scrapbooks. Concord, Mass. Celebrations Scrapbook Collection. Vault A15, Unit A1. William Munroe Special Collections, CFPL.

Parini, Jay. *Robert Frost: A Life.* New York: Holt, 1999.

Smigel, Libby. "Mackaye, Percy." *American National Biography.* 1999.

**The Whipping Post Elm: A Tree of Mythic Proportions:**

Concord (MA). "Report of the Tree Warden." *Annual Report of the Officers of the Town of Concord, Massachusetts for the Year Ending December 31, 1941.* Concord: The Town, 1942. 38.

"Emerson Elm Planted in 1776, Shown by Historical Records. Judge John S. Keyes Authority for Statement Recently Published in *Herald*—No Reason Why Facts Should Be Disputed." *The Concord Herald* 1 Sept. 1932: 1.

French, Allen. Town House Elm file, 1932. Allen French Papers. Vault A45, French Unit 1, Box 1, Folder 18. William Munroe Special Collections, CFPL.

"Historic Old Elm Cut Down in Concord." *Concord Enterprise* 30 July 1941: 1.

Lawes, Lewis E. "Flogging." *Dictionary of American History.* 2nd ed., rev. 1942.

Moore, John H. "The Town House Elm: When and by Whom Planted?" *The Concord Journal* 25 Aug. 1932: 1–2.

"The Old Elm on Concord Common." *The Monitor* (Concord, MA) 21 June 1862: 64.

Shipton, Clifford K. "Whipping Post, The." *Dictionary of American History.* 2nd ed., rev. 1942.

Swayne, Josephine Latham. *The Story of Concord Told by American Writers.* Boston: E.F. Worcester P, 1906.

Thoreau, Henry David. Journal entry for 11 June 1852. *The Journals of Henry D. Thoreau.* Ed. Bradford Torrey and Francis H. Allen. Boston: Houghton Mifflin, 1906.

# II. CHANGE HAPPENS

**Introduction:**

Concord Free Public Library. Exhibition text for the display *Concord Bygones,* 2001. Comp. Leslie Perrin Wilson. Concord Free Public Library Records, Series VIII, Subseries C. William Munroe Special Collections, CFPL.

**A Moving Story:**

Concord Historical Commission. *Survey of Historical and Architectural Resources, Concord, Massachusetts.* Rev. ed. Concord: The Commission, 2002.

Curtis, John Obed. *Moving Historic Buildings.* Lexington, SC: International Association of Structural Movers, 1991.

"How to Move Houses." *American Agriculturist* 32 (1873): 417–18.

Jarvis, Edward. *Houses and People in Concord* (transcribed from Jarvis's 1882 ms. and annotated by Adams Tolman). Ts., 1915. William Munroe Special Collections, CFPL.

Keyes, John Shepard. *Houses, & Owners or Occupants in Concord, 1885* (annotated by Adams Tolman; typed and further annotated by Marian B. Miller). Ts., 1940. William Munroe Special Collections, CFPL.

Stevenson, David. *Sketch of the Civil Engineering of North America. Comprising Remarks on the Harbours, River and Lake Navigation, Water-Works, Canals, Roads, Railways, Bridges, and Other Works in That Country.* London: J. Weale, 1838.

Thoreau, Henry David. Journal entries for 11, 13, and 14 Mar. 1859. *The Journals.*

Wheeler, Ruth Robinson. Concord House Files. William Munroe Special Collections, CFPL.

**Williamsburg on the Mill Dam: The Gowen Proposal, 1928:**

Concord (MA). *Names of Persons in the Town of Concord. Listed in accordance with Chapter 51, Section 4, General Laws.* Concord: Board of Assessors, 1927–37.

Concord Historical Commission. *Survey of Historical and Architectural Resources.* 4: 368/374 Sudbury Road; 4: 557 Sudbury Road.

Concord Mill Dam Company. Records, 1826–54. Vault A25, Unit 15. William Munroe Special Collections, CFPL.

Concord Mill Dam Company. Records, 1836–54. Nathan Brooks Papers. Vault A45, Brooks Unit 1, Box 17a, Folder 6. William Munroe Special Collections, CFPL.

"Concord Milldam to Be Transformed—Old Buildings to Give Way to Unique Plan." *The Concord Journal* 14 June 1928: 1–2.

Cook, Marion F. Letter to the editor. *The Concord Journal* 12 July 1928: 3.

Eaton, Richard J. Letter to the editor. *The Concord Journal* 28 June 1928: 1–2.

"Gowen, Albert Younglove." *Harvard Alumni Directory.* Cambridge: Harvard U, 1937. 444.

"Gowen Trade Board Speaker. Tells of Plans for a Dream of Transfigured Mill Dam." *Concord Enterprise* 10 Oct. 1928: 3.

Holm, Donald. "Hi Jinks on the *Speejacks*." *The Circumnavigators: Small Boat Voyagers of Modern Times.* New York: Prentice-Hall, 1974.

Masthead. *The Concord Journal* 3 Jan. 1929: 4.

"The Milldam Enterprise Is Revived. Board of Trade Approves Mr. Gowen's Plan." *The Concord Journal* 11 Oct. 1928: 1.

"Mr. Gowen Withdraws from Milldam. Sees No Hope for Local Improvement." *The Concord Journal* 12 Dec. 1929: 1.

Pierce, Frank. "Milldam Property Will Not Be Sold." *The Concord Journal* 5 July 1928: 1.

"A Survey of Mr. Gowen's Proposal for the Milldam. The Pro's and Con's [sic] as *The Journal* Finds Them." *The Concord Journal* 21 June 1928: 1–2.

Wood, Charles G. Letter to the editor. *The Concord Journal* 28 June 1928: 5.

Yetter, George Humphrey. *Williamsburg Before and After: The Rebirth of Virginia's Colonial Capital.* Williamsburg, VA: Colonial Williamsburg Foundation, 1988.

**The United Nations in Concord? "My How the Fur Flew":**
Abbott, Mary Ogden. Letter to the editor. *The Concord Journal* 10 Jan. 1946: 1.

Bygrave, H.R. Letter to the editor. *The Concord Journal* 3 Jan. 1946: 1, 8.

Conant, Wallace B. Letter to the editor. *The Concord Journal* 3 Jan. 1946: 8.

"Concord Is Logical Site for the UNO." *The Concord Journal* 20 Dec. 1945: 1.

"Concord Seeks UNO Site Here. Mansfield Legion Post Commends Action of Cong. Edith Nourse Rogers." *Concord Enterprise* 3 Jan. 1946: 1.

French, Allen. Letter to the editor. *The Concord Journal* 27 Dec. 1945: 4.

Hoar, Samuel. Letter to the editor. *The Concord Journal* 27 Dec. 1945: 4.

Krasno, Jean. "A Step Along an Evolutionary Path: The Founding of the United Nations." *United Nations Studies at Yale.* 24 Nov. 2000 *http://www.yale.edu/unsy/Oralhist/krasno/intro.html.*

"Origin and History of the United Nations." 24 Nov. 2000 *http://members.dencity.com/bpolsky/origin.html.*

Rideout, Gertrude. "The Host." *The Concord Journal* 10 Jan. 1946: 8.

Robbins, Roland Wells. Letter to the editor. *The Concord Journal* 10 Jan. 1946: 8.

"Stedman Buttrick Offers Land for U.N.O. Location." *The Concord Journal* 3 Jan. 1946: 1.

"Sudbury, Concord Area Suitable for U.N.O. Home Site." *Concord Enterprise* 24 Jan. 1946: 1, 4.

"United Nations. History and development." *Encyclopaedia Britannica.* 24 Nov. 2000 *http://www.britannica.com/bcom/eb/article/6/0,5716,115666+3,00.html.*

"UNO Aim Excludes Hyde Park Village." *The New York Times* 19 Jan. 1946: 8.

"UNO Group Views Sites from Blimp." *The New York Times* 21 Jan. 1946: 3.

Walker, William. "Concord Nominated as Site of UNO Capital." *The Concord Journal* 15 Nov. 1945: 1,8.

Wheeler, Ruth Robinson. "Will Change Spoil Us?"

**Concord's Lost Canopy of Elms:**

Benvie, Sam. "American Elm, White Elm, Gray Elm, Water Elm, Swamp Elm." *Encyclopedia of North American Trees.* Buffalo, NY: Firefly Books, 2000. 269–70.

Concord (MA). "Department of Natural Resources." *The Annual Report of the Town of Concord, Massachusetts for the Year Ending in December, 1967.* Concord: The Town, 1968. 121–22.

Concord (MA). "Forestry Division." *The Annual Report of the Officers of the Town of Concord, Massachusetts* (for the years 1960, 1964–66). Concord: The Town, 1961, 1965–67.

Concord (MA). "Report of Committee on Dutch Elm Disease." *The Annual Report of the Officers of the Town of Concord, Massachusetts from January 1, 1934 to December 31, 1934.* Concord: The Town, 1935. 27.

Concord (MA). "Report of the Tree Warden." *Annual Reports of the Town Officers of Concord, Mass.* (for the years 1901–04, 1906–08, 1910–11, 1933, 1942). Concord: The Town, 1902–05, 1907–09, 1911–12, 1934, 1943.

Concord (MA). "Tree Division." *The Annual Report of the Town of Concord, Massachusetts* (for the years 1968, 1970, 1974–78). Concord: The Town, 1969, 1971, 1975–79.

Concord Ornamental Tree Society. Records, 1833–37 (photocopied). Concord Pamphlet 65, Item 21. William Munroe Special Collections, CFPL.

"Dutch elm disease." *The New Encyclopaedia Britannica. Micropaedia.* 15th ed. 1998.

Joslin, Elmer. "Elm Street." *Notes on the Acceptances or Layouts of Public Ways in the Town of Concord, 1956.* Ts. William Munroe Special Collections, CFPL.

Munroe, Alfred. *Concord Out of Door Sketches.* Concord: Érudite P, 1903.

Thoreau, Henry David. Journal entry, 1850 (date unspecified). *The Journals.* 2:53.

## III. A VIGOROUS COMMUNITY SPIRIT

**Introduction:**

Bartlett, George Bradford. *Concord Historic, Literary and Picturesque.* 16th ed., rev. Boston: Lothrop Pub. Co., 1895.

Concord (MA). "Boards and Committees." *Annual Report of the Town of Concord, Massachusetts for the Year Ending December 2005.* Concord: The Town, 2006. 1–4.

Concord (MA). "Report of the Board of Selectmen." *Annual Report of the Officers of the Town of Concord, Massachusetts for the Year Ending December 31st 1956.* Concord: The Town, 1957. 23–29.

Concord Committee of Arrangements for the Second Centennial Celebration of the Incorporation of Concord. Records, 1835. Vault A15, Unit B1. William Munroe Special Collections, CFPL.

Concord Female Charitable Society. Records, 1814–1943. Vault A75, Con. Fem., Unit 1. William Munroe Special Collections, CFPL.

Concord Lyceum. Records, 1828–1928. Vault A75, Con. Lyc., Unit 1. William Munroe Special Collections, CFPL.

Concord Soldiers' Aid Society. Records, 1861–65. Vault A75, Con. Sol., Unit 1. William Munroe Special Collections, CFPL.

Emerson, Ralph Waldo. *A Historical Discourse.*

French, Allen. "William Henry Hunt." *Memoirs of Members of the Social Circle in Concord.* Fifth Series. Concord: The Circle, 1940. 251–67.

**Mary Minot's "Widow's Thirds":**

*Boundaries of the Widow Mary Minot's thirds set off April 17, 1813.* Ms. Miscellaneous Property Documents (Primarily Deeds) Relating Mainly to Concord (Mass.). Vault A50, Unit 4, Folder 4. William Munroe Special Collections, CFPL.

Concord (MA). *Concord, Massachusetts Births, Marriages, and Deaths, 1635–1850.* Concord: The Town, 1895.

Concord Historical Commission. *Survey of Historical and Architectural Resources.* 2: 201 Lexington Road.

"Dower." *Encyclopedia.com.* 17 June 2004 *http://www.encyclopedia.com /html/dl/dower.asp.*

"Griffith v. Griffith's Executors: 1798." *Gale Free Resources. Women's History Month. Women's Rights on Trial.* 24 June 2004 *http://www.galegroup .com/free_resources/whm/trials/griffith.htm.*

Harding, Walter. *The Days of Henry Thoreau.* New York: Knopf, 1965.

*An inventory of Capt. J. Minot's Real estate.* Ms. Miscellaneous Property Documents (Primarily Deeds) Relating Mainly to Concord (Mass.). Vault A50, Unit 4, Folder 4. William Munroe Special Collections, CFPL.

Larkin, Jack. "A Brief Note on Inheritance," 1980. *Old Sturbridge Village Online Resource Library.* 24 June 2004 *http://www.osv.org/learning /DocumentViewer.php?DocID=736.*

"Marriage and Family." *Life in Elizabethan England.* 24 June 2004 *http://renaissance.dm.net/compendium/10.htm.*

"Massachusetts Intestate Succession Laws." *Financial Planning Toolkit.* 18 July 2004 *http://www.finance.cch.com/pops/c50s10d190_MA.asp.*

Ripley, Ezra. Letter, "To the most Worshipful Benj. Russell Esq[r]. Grand master, other officers & members of the Grand Lodge of Massachusetts," 28 July 1815. Ms. Ezra Ripley Papers. Vault A30, Unit B4, Folder 1. William Munroe Special Collections, CFPL.

Salmon, Marylynn. "Women, Legal Status of." *The Encyclopedia of Colonial and Revolutionary America.* Ed. John Mack Faragher. New York: Da Capo P, 1996. 461–62.

Thoreau, Henry David. "Chesuncook." *The Maine Woods.* Boston: Houghton Mifflin, 1906. 93–173.

Wheeler, Joseph C. "Where Thoreau Was Born." *Concord Saunterer* ns 7 (1999): 5–12.

**Christmas in Concord, 1853:**

Concord (MA). *Concord, Massachusetts Births, Marriages, and Deaths.*

Emerson, Lidian. Letter to Ellen Tucker Emerson, 11 Dec. 1853. *The Selected Letters of Lidian Jackson Emerson.* Ed. Delores Bird Carpenter. Columbia: U Missouri P, 1987. 191–92.

Hoar, Ebenezer Rockwood. "Memoir of William Whiting." *Memoirs of Members of the Social Circle in Concord.* Second Series. 247–65.

Hoar, Elizabeth. Letter to Elizabeth Palmer Peabody, 30 Dec. 1853. "Elizabeth of Concord: Selected Letters of Elizabeth Sherman Hoar (1814–1878) to the Emersons, Family, and the Emerson Circle (Part Three)." Ed. Elizabeth Maxfield-Miller. *Studies in the American Renaissance* (1986): 176–77.

Hoar, George Frisbie. *A Boy Sixty Years Ago.* Boston: Perry Mason, 1898.

Hudson, Bessie Keyes. "Mrs. Woodward Hudson's Memoir of Mrs. Ebenezer Rockwood Hoar." Ed. Leslie Perrin Wilson. *Concord Saunterer* ns 9 (2001): 87–125.

Hunt, William Henry. "A Concord Farmer Looks Back: The Reminiscences of William Henry Hunt." Ed. Leslie Perrin Wilson. *Concord Saunterer* ns 10 (2002): 65–123.

Nissenbaum, Stephen W. *Christmas in Early New England, 1620–1820: Puritanism, Popular Culture, and the Printed Word.* Worcester: American Antiquarian Soc., 1996.

Thoreau, Henry David. Journal entries for 22 and 24 Dec. 1853. *The Journals.*

W., A.M. "Christmas in Concord." Article, 26 Dec. 1853, clipped from *The Commonwealth* (Boston) and scrapbooked by Samuel Ripley Bartlett. Bartlett Family Papers. Vault A45, Bartlett Unit 1, Box 1, Folder 6. William Munroe Special Collections, CFPL.

**Fire at the Emerson House, 1872:**

"The *Boston Daily Advertiser,* July 25, 1872" (footnote 86, containing extracts from article in *Advertiser*). *The Letters of Ralph Waldo Emerson.* Ed. Ralph L. Rusk. New York: Columbia UP, 1939. 6:214.

Cabot, James Elliot. *A Memoir of Ralph Waldo Emerson.* Cambridge: Riverside P, 1887.

Committee on Reception of R.W. Emerson. *A Public Reception of Mr. R.W. Emerson on His Return Home from Europe Will be given by the citizens of Concord* (broadside). Broadside and Poster Collection, 1873 May 27. William Munroe Special Collections, CFPL.

Committee on Reception of R.W. Emerson. Records, 1873. Vault A15, Unit D5. William Munroe Special Collections, CFPL.

Emerson, Edward Waldo. Annotation to 24 July 1872 journal entry by Ralph Waldo Emerson. *Ralph Waldo Emerson. Journals, 1864–1876* (Vol. 10 of *Journals of Ralph Waldo Emerson*). Ed. Edward Waldo Emerson and Waldo Emerson Forbes. Cambridge: Riverside P, 1914. 386–92.

Emerson, Edward Waldo. *Emerson in Concord. A Memoir Written for the "Social Circle" in Concord.* Boston: Houghton Mifflin, 1888.

Emerson, Ellen Tucker. *The Letters of Ellen Tucker Emerson.* Ed. Edith E.W. Gregg. Kent, OH: Kent State UP, 1982.

Emerson, Ellen Tucker. *The Life of Lidian Jackson Emerson.* Ed. Delores Bird Carpenter. East Lansing: Michigan State UP, 1992.

Emerson, Lidian Jackson. *The Selected Letters.*

Emerson, Ralph Waldo. Letter to Concord Fire Department, 29 July 1872 (transcribed). *Record-Book of Fountain Engine Co. No. 1, 1871 to 1874. Concord Fire Department.* Ms. William Munroe Special Collections, CFPL.

Emerson, Ralph Waldo. "New England Reformers." *Essays: Second Series* (Vol. 3 of *The Complete Works of Ralph Waldo Emerson*). Cambridge: Riverside P, 1883. 249–85.

McAleer, John. *Ralph Waldo Emerson: Days of Encounter.* Boston: Little, Brown, 1984.

Rusk, Ralph L. *The Life of Ralph Waldo Emerson.* New York: Scribner's, 1949.

**William Munroe's Concord Free Public Library:**

Alexander, Edward P. "Historical Prologue: The Rise of American History Museums." *Leadership for the Future: Changing Directorial Roles in American History Museums and Historical Societies. Collected Essays.* Ed. Bryant F. Tolles, Jr. Nashville, TN: American Assn. for State and Local History, 1991. 5–19.

Bartlett, George Bradford. *Concord Guide Book.* Boston: D. Lothrop, 1880. (The chapter titled "Free Public Library" was based on information supplied to Bartlett by Alfred Munroe.)

Committee on the Widening of Main Street. Records, 1871–72. Vault A5, Unit A9. William Munroe Special Collections, CFPL.

Committee on the Widening of Main Street. "The Widening of Main Street." *Annual Reports of the Officers of the Town of Concord from March 1, 1871, to March 1, 1872.* Concord: The Town, 1872. 44–48.

Concord Free Public Library. *Dedication of the New Building for the Free Public Library of Concord, Massachusetts, Wednesday, Oct. 1, 1873.* Boston: Tolman & White, 1873.

Concord Free Public Library. Exhibition text for the display *William Munroe's Vision,* 1998. Comp. Leslie Perrin Wilson. Concord Free Public Library Records, Series VIII, Subseries A. William Munroe Special Collections, CFPL.

Concord Free Public Library. Records, 1846–<present> (bulk 1873–<present>). Vault A60, Unit D1. William Munroe Special Collections, CFPL.

Concord Free Public Library Corporation. "Report of the Trustees of the Free Public Library." *Annual Reports of the Selectmen and Other Officers of the Town of Concord, from March 1, 1873, to March 1, 1874.* Concord: The Town, 1874. 56–63.

Concord Historical Commission. *Survey of Historical and Architectural Resources.* 2: 45 Hubbard Street.

Concord Town Library. Records, 1851–73. Vault A60, Unit C1. William Munroe Special Collections, CFPL.

Concord Town Library Committee. "The Library. Report of the Town Committee." *Annual Reports of the Selectmen and Other Officers of the Town of Concord, from March 1, 1873, to March 1, 1874.* Concord: The Town, 1874. 44–55.

Concord Town Meeting. Minutes, 1851–76. Vol. D1–12. Concord Town Archives, CFPL.

Munroe, William. Papers, 1861–75. Vault A45, Munroe Unit 1. William Munroe Special Collections, CFPL.

Obituaries of William Munroe, from *Christian Register* and *Boston Evening Transcript*, Apr. and May 1877. Obituary Scrapbooks, Concord, Mass. Vault B15, Unit 2. William Munroe Special Collections, CFPL. 1:29, and insert between 1:30 and 1:31.

Smith, Henry F. "Alfred Munroe." *Memoirs of Members of the Social Circle in Concord.* Fourth Series. Concord: The Circle, 1909. 294–306.

## IV. WHAT MAKES A CONCORDIAN?

**Introduction:**

Bushman, Claudia L. *"A Good Poor Man's Wife": Being a Chronicle of Harriet Hanson Robinson and Her Family in Nineteenth-Century New England.* Hanover, NH: UP of New England, 1981.

DeSuze, Carl. *Honored Citizens,* 1988. Ts. Collection of Materials Issued by or Relating to the Public Ceremonies and Celebrations Committee, Concord, Mass. Concord Pamphlet 48, Item G4. William Munroe Special Collections, CFPL.

Emerson, Ralph Waldo. *A Historical Discourse.*

Hoar, George Frisbie. *A Boy Sixty Years Ago.*

Jarvis, Edward. *Supposed Decay of Families in New England Disproved by the Experience of the People of Concord, Mass.* Boston: P of David Clapp & Son, 1884. Original printing: *The New-England Historical and Genealogical Register* 38 (1884): 385–95.

**Whatever Happened to Benjamin Cheney?:**
"Benjamin Cheney." *FamilySearch.* 31 Jan. 2001 *http://www.familysearch .com/Eng/Search/af/individual_record.asp?recid=7370240.*

Bond, Henry. *Genealogies of the Families and Descendants of the Early Settlers of Watertown, Massachusetts, Including Waltham and Weston; to Which Is Appended The Early History of the Town.* Boston: Little, Brown, 1855.

Cambridge (MA). *Vital Records of Cambridge, Massachusetts to the Year 1850.* Comp. Thomas W. Baldwin. Boston: Wright & Potter Print. Co., 1914–15.

Charlestown (MA). *Vital Records of Charlestown, Massachusetts to the Year 1850.* Boston: New England Historic Genealogical Soc., 1984.

Concord (MA). *Concord, Massachusetts Births, Marriages, and Deaths.*

Concord (MA). Town Records, 1655–1823. Ms. transcripts. Vault A5, Unit A8. William Munroe Special Collections, CFPL. Notebooks 3, 4.

Concord Historical Commission. *Survey of Historical and Architectural Resources.* 2: 5/7, 13/15 Lexington Road.

Fischer, David Hackett. *Albion's Seed: Four British Folkways in America.* New York: Oxford UP, 1989.

Furer, Rebecca. "The Cheney Family." *Connecticut History Online.* 31 Jan. 2001 *http://www.lib.uconn.edu/cho/Education/twofamilies/cheney.htm.*

"Marriages in Glastonbury, CT." 31 Jan. 2001 *http://pages.prodigy .net/kathyb/glasmar2.htm.*

Middlesex County Court of General Sessions of the Peace. Record Book, 1692–1723. Massachusetts Supreme Judicial Court Archives, Boston, MA.

Page, Mercy, and Daniel Pellett. Document (ms.) apprenticing Benjamin Cheney to Daniel Pellett, 22 June 1699. Concord Document Collection. Box 1, 1699 folder. William Munroe Special Collections, CFPL.

Pope, Charles Henry. *The Cheney Genealogy.* Boston: The Author, 1897.

"Susanna Pellett." *FamilySearch.* 31 Jan. 2001 *http://www.familysearch .com/Eng/Search/PRF/individual_record_prf.asp?recid=180205012.*

Thompson, Roger. *Sex in Middlesex: Popular Mores in a Massachusetts County, 1649–1699.* Amherst: U Massachusetts P, 1986.

Watertown (MA). *Watertown Records: Comprising the Third Book of Town Proceedings and the Second Book of Births, Marriages and Deaths to End of 1737. Also Plan and Register of Burials in Arlington Street Burying Ground. Prepared for Publication by the Historical Society.* Watertown: P of Fred G. Barker, 1900.

Wheeler, Ruth Robinson. Concord House File L3 (Pellett/Barrett/D.A.R. Chapter House).

Wheeler, Ruth Robinson. "D.A.R. Chapter House." *The Concord Journal* 24 Mar. 1938: 8.

Wheeler, Ruth Robinson. *Our American Mile.* Concord: Concord Antiquarian Soc., 1957.

**Wilkie, Bob, and Ned: The James Family in Concord:**
Collection of Materials Issued by or Relating to the Concord School (of Franklin B. Sanborn), Concord, Mass., 1858–1861. Concord Pamphlet 55, Item B1. William Munroe Special Collections, CFPL.

Concord directories (printed; residential/business) for the years 1886, 1892, 1896, 1901, 1905–6, 1909–10, 1917, 1921. Places of publication and publishers vary.

Concord Historical Commission. *Survey of Historical and Architectural Resources.* 2: 70 Lexington Road; 4: 105 Walden Street; 4: 49 Sudbury Road.

Events in Concord Scrapbooks, 1852–1985. Vault B15, Unit 1. William Munroe Special Collections, CFPL. 2 (1872–1921; bulk 1915–21); 3 (1855–1927; bulk 1921–27); 4 (1865–1932; bulk 1927–32); 6 (1854–1944; bulk 1937–44).

Feinstein, Howard M. *Becoming William James.* Ithaca: Cornell UP, 1984.

Habegger, Alfred. "James, Henry [Sr.]." *American National Biography.* 1999.

Haralson, Eric L. "James, Henry, Jr."; "James, Henry, Sr."; "James, William." *Biographical Dictionary of Transcendentalism.* Westport, CT: Greenwood P, 1996.

James, Alice. *The Death and Letters of Alice James: Selected Correspondence.* Ed. Ruth Bernard Yeazell. Berkeley: U California P, 1981.

James, Edward Holton. *I Am a Yankee.* Concord, MA: Yankee Freemen Movement, 1943.

Kelly, Alan. "James, Alice." *American National Biography.* 1999.

Keyes, John Shepard. *Houses, & Owners or Occupants in Concord, 1885.*

Maher, Jane. *Biography of Broken Fortunes: Wilkie and Bob, Brothers of William, Henry, and Alice James.* Hamden, CT: Archon Books, 1986.

Miller, Marian B. *A Concord Yankee,* 1978. Ts. Concord Pamphlet 43, James 10. William Munroe Special Collections, CFPL.

Obituary Scrapbooks, Concord, Mass., 1840–1963. 2 (1892–1930); 4 (1953–63).

Powers, Lyall H. "James, Henry [Jr.]." *American National Biography.* 1999.

Skrupskelis, Ignas K. "James, William." *American National Biography.* 1999.

**William Henry Hunt, from Punkatasset to Paris:**
*Commemorative Reunion of the Name and Family of Hunt, at Town Hall, Concord, Mass., August 12, 1885. Being the 250th Anniversary of Its American Pioneer, William Hunt's Settlement at Concord, and Its Recognition by His Descendants, Alliances, and Others* (printed program).

Concord (MA). Annual town reports (variously titled), for multiple years between 1844/45 and 1988. Concord: The Town, 1845–1989.

Concord (MA). Assessors' valuations, 1825–1910. Concord Town Archives, CFPL.

Concord (MA). *Concord, Massachusetts Births, Marriages, and Deaths.*

Concord Farmers' Club. Records, 1852–83. Vault A10, Unit 3. William Munroe Special Collections, CFPL.

Concord Historical Commission. *Survey of Historical and Architectural Resources.* 3: 709 Monument Street; 712 Monument Street; 754 Monument Street.

Concord School Committee. *The Annual Report of the School Committee of Concord, Mass.,* for multiple years between 1869/70 and 1900/01. Concord: The Town, 1870–1901.

Donahue, Brian. "The Forests and Fields of Concord: An Ecological History, 1750–1850." *Concord: The Social History of a New England Town, 1750–1850.* Ed. David Hackett Fischer. Waltham, MA: Brandeis U, 1983. 15–63.

French, Allen. Correspondence with William Henry Hunt and working papers for French's Social Circle memoir of Hunt, including a letter from Hunt's niece Mary R. Jacobs and Jacobs's responses to the Social Circle biographical questionnaire on Hunt. Allen French Papers. Box 6. Minute Man National Historical Park Archives, Concord, MA.

French, Allen. "William Henry Hunt."

Gross, Robert A. "Culture and Cultivation: Agriculture and Society in Thoreau's Concord." *Journal of American History* 69:1 (1982): 42–61.

Hawthorne, Nathaniel. *The American Notebooks.* Ed. Claude M. Simpson. Columbus: Ohio State UP, 1972.

Hunt, William Henry. "A Concord Farmer Looks Back."

"A Melancholy Suicide." *Concord Freeman* 11 July 1845:2.

Middlesex Agricultural Society. Records, 1803–93. Vault A10, Unit 4. William Munroe Special Collections, CFPL.

Obituary Scrapbooks, Concord, Mass., 1840–1963. 2 (1892–1930).

Russell, Howard S. *A Long, Deep Furrow: Three Centuries of Farming in New England.* Abr. and with a foreword by Mark Lapping. Hanover, NH: UP of New England, 1982.

United States Census Office. Seventh Census, 1850. Alphabetical card file of transcribed Concord names. William Munroe Special Collections, CFPL.

United States Census Office. Eighth Census, 1860. Alphabetical card file of transcribed Concord names. William Munroe Special Collections, CFPL.

United States Census Office. Twelfth Census, 1900. Middlesex County, MA listings, inc. Concord. Microfilm.

Wheeler, Ruth Robinson. Concord House Files.

Wheeler, Ruth Robinson. *North Bridge Neighbors: A History of Area B, Minute Man National Historical Park,* 1964. Ts. William Munroe Special Collections, CFPL.

**Theodore Baker:**
"Baker, Theodore." *Baker's Biographical Dictionary of Musicians.* 8th ed. 1991.

Billings, Eleanor Motley. "Music in the Meeting House." *The Meeting House on the Green: A History of the First Parish in Concord and Its Church.* Ed. John Whittemore Teele. Concord: The First Parish, 1985.

Concord (MA). *Concord, Massachusetts Births, Marriages, and Deaths.*

Concord (MA). Transcribed birth, marriage, and death cards, 1851–1935. William Munroe Special Collections, CFPL.

Concord Female Charitable Society. Records, 1814–1943.

First Parish in Concord. Records of Music in the Church, 1812–1928. First Parish in Concord Records. Vault A30, Unit A1, Series X. William Munroe Special Collections, CFPL.

Framingham (MA). Vital record cards. Framingham Town Clerk's Office, Framingham, MA.

French, Allen. "William Henry Hunt."

Hitchcock, H. Wiley. "Baker, Theodore." *The New Grove Dictionary of Music and Musicians.* 2nd ed. 2001.

Hunt, William Henry. "A Concord Farmer Looks Back."

Jacobs, Mary R. Responses to Social Circle biographical questionnaire on William Henry Hunt, and related materials. Box 6. Minute Man National Historical Park Archives.

Keyes, John Shepard. *Houses, & Owners or Occupants in Concord, 1885.*

Middlesex Agricultural Society. Records, 1803–93.

Simmons, Edward Emerson. *From Seven to Seventy: Memories of a Painter and A Yankee.* New York: Harper, 1922.

Trinitarian Congregational Church. Record Book 2, 1868–1902. Trinitarian Congregational Church Archives. William Munroe Special Collections, CFPL.

United States Census Office. Eighth Census, 1860. Alphabetical card file of transcribed Concord names.

## V. HIGHER CONCERNS

**Introduction:**
Emerson, Ralph Waldo. "Hamatreya." *Ralph Waldo Emerson. Collected Poems and Translations.* New York: Library of America, 1994. 28–29.

Emerson, Ralph Waldo. *A Historical Discourse.*

Riverbend Landing, Inc. *A Resource Guide for the Spirit: Concord/Carlisle, Massachusetts.* Concord: Riverbend Landing, 2000.

**Slaveholding and Abolition in One Concord Family:**
Brooks, George M. "Memoir of Tilly Merrick." *Memoirs of Members of the Social Circle in Concord.* Second Series. 58–62.

Concord (MA). *Concord, Massachusetts Births, Marriages, and Deaths.*

Concord Female Charitable Society. Records, 1814–1943.

Concord Ladies' Antislavery Society. Records, 1853–64. Vault A75, Lad. Ant. Unit 1. William Munroe Special Collections, CFPL.

Concord Soldiers' Aid Society. Records, 1861–65.

Hudson, Bessie Keyes. "Mrs. Woodward Hudson's Memoir of Mrs. Ebenezer Rockwood Hoar."

Jarvis, Edward. "Company of Exempts, 1814." *Traditions and Reminiscences of Concord, Massachusetts, 1779–1878.* 25.

Merrick, George Byron. *Genealogy of the Merrick-Mirick-Myrick Family of Massachusetts, 1636–1902.* Madison, WI: Tracy, Gibbs, 1902.

Merrick, Tilly. Papers, 1777–1853 (bulk 1781–1836). Nathan Brooks Papers. Vault A45, Brooks Unit 1, Series VI. William Munroe Special Collections, CFPL.

Middlesex County Antislavery Society. Records, 1834–51. Vault A75, Mid. C.A. Unit 1. William Munroe Special Collections, CFPL.

Petrulionis, Sandra Harbert. "'Swelling That Great Tide of Humanity': The Concord, Massachusetts, Female Anti-Slavery Society." *New England Quarterly* 74:3 (2001): 385–418.

Robinson, William S. *"Warrington" Pen-Portraits: A Collection of Personal and Political Reminiscences from 1848 to 1876, from the Writings of William S. Robinson.* Ed. H.J.H. Robinson. Boston: Mrs. W.S. Robinson, 1877.

United States Census Office. Seventh Census, 1850. Alphabetical card file of transcribed Concord names.

United States Census Office. Eighth Census, 1860. Alphabetical card file of transcribed Concord names.

Women's Parish Association. Records, 1881–1983. First Parish in Concord Records. Vault A30, Unit A1, Series IV.

**"Taps in the Wall, & Thumps in the Table-Drawer":**

Bosco, Ronald A. "Spiritualism." *Encyclopedia of Transcendentalism.* Westport, CT: Greenwood P, 1996. 204–07.

Concord (MA). Assessors' valuations, 1836–65.

Concord (MA). *Concord, Massachusetts Births, Marriages, and Deaths.*

Emerson, Edward Waldo. "Page 209, note 1" (footnote to passage in Ralph Waldo Emerson's "Worship"). *The Conduct of Life* (Vol. 6 of *The Complete Works of Ralph Waldo Emerson*). Cambridge: Riverside P, 1904. 391.

Emerson, Ralph Waldo. *Emerson in His Journals.* Ed. Joel Porte. Cambridge: Belknap P of Harvard UP, 1982.

Emerson, Ralph Waldo. "Worship." *The Conduct of Life* (Vol. 6 of *The Complete Works of Ralph Waldo Emerson*). Cambridge: Riverside P, 1904. 199–242.

Kerr, Howard. *Mediums, and Spirit-Rappers, and Roaring Radicals: Spiritualism in American Literature, 1850–1900.* Urbana: U Illinois P, 1972.

Merrick, Augustus. Papers, 1831–58. Nathan Brooks Papers. Series VI, Subseries G.

Merrick, George Byron. *Genealogy of the Merrick-Mirick-Myrick Family.*

Ronda, Bruce A. *Elizabeth Palmer Peabody: A Reformer on Her Own Terms.* Cambridge: Harvard UP, 1999.

Storey, Moorfield, and Edward Waldo Emerson. *Ebenezer Rockwood Hoar: A Memoir.* Boston: Houghton Mifflin, 1911.

Thoreau, Henry David. *Familiar Letters.* Ed. F.B. Sanborn. Boston: Houghton Mifflin, 1906.

Thoreau, Henry David. *Journal. Volume 4: 1851–1852.* Ed. Robert Sattelmeyer. Princeton, NJ: Princeton UP, 1992.

**H.W.S. Cleveland, Designer of Sleepy Hollow:**

Bartlett, George Bradford. *Concord Guide Book.*

Cleveland, Horace William Shaler. *A Few Words on the Arrangement of Rural Cemeteries.* Chicago: Geo. K. Hazlitt, 1881.

Collection of Materials Issued by or Relating to the Cemetery Committee of Concord, Mass., <1849–2001>. Concord Pamphlet 48, Item E1. William Munroe Special Collections, CFPL.

Collection of Materials Relating to the National Register Nomination of Sleepy Hollow Cemetery, <1998>. Concord Pamphlet 48, Item E1d. William Munroe Special Collections, CFPL.

Concord (MA). "Expenditures. Cemetery." *Reports of the Selectmen, Overseers of the Poor, and Other Town Officers, Relative to the Expenses of the Town of Concord, for the Year 1855, '56.* Concord: The Town, 1856. 10–11.

Concord Historical Commission. *Survey of Historical and Architectural Resources.* 1: Bedford Street—Sleepy Hollow Cemetery (filed at 24 Court Lane).

Concord Lyceum. Records, 1828–1928.

Emerson, Ralph Waldo. "Address to the Inhabitants of Concord at the Consecration of Sleepy Hollow, September 29, 1855." *Miscellanies* (Vol. 11 of *The Complete Works of Ralph Waldo Emerson*). Cambridge: Riverside P, 1904. 427–36.

Keyes, John Shepard. Autobiography, 1821–66. Ms. John Shepard Keyes Papers. Vault A45, Keyes Unit 2, Series I. William Munroe Special Collections, CFPL.

Nadenicek, Daniel J. "Sleepy Hollow Cemetery: Philosophy Made Substance." *Emerson Society Papers* 5:1 (1994): 1, 2, 8.

Nadenicek, Daniel J., William H. Tishler, and Lance M. Neckar. "Cleveland, Horace William Shaler"; "Copeland, Robert Morris." *Pioneers of American Landscape Design.* New York: McGraw-Hill, 2000.

**Philosophy and Toadstools:**

"An aged philosopher . . . " (brief notice of Abby Pratt's poisoning by toadstool). *Concord Freeman* 5 Aug. 1887: 1.

Barrett Collection of Printed Ephemera Relating to Sessions of the Concord School of Philosophy, Concord, Mass., 1879–88. Vault A35, A.B. Alcott Unit 2. William Munroe Special Collections, CFPL.

Bartlett, George Bradford. *Concord Historic, Literary and Picturesque.*

Harris, William Torrey. Concord School of Philosophy Scrapbook, 1879–87. Vault A35, W.T. Harris Unit 2. William Munroe Special Collections, CFPL.

Myerson, Joel. "Concord School of Philosophy." *Encyclopedia of Transcendentalism.* 41–42.

Pratt, Abby. Letter to William Torrey Harris, 16 May 1887. Ms. Letters to William Torrey Harris. Vault A35, W.T. Harris Unit 1, Folder 7. William Munroe Special Collections, CFPL.

# INDEX

Town House Elm: see under
  Whipping Post Elm
Town meeting: 38, 46, 52, 53, 64
Traditions, local: xiii, 29, 60, 62
Transcendentalism: xii, 13, 30, 46,
  66, 79, 89, 91–94
Transcendentalists: xi, xiv, 1, 6, 44,
  45, 46, 66, 80, 81, 91–94; see also
  under Alcott, Emerson, Peabody,
  Thoreau
Tree planting: 33, 36
Tree Warden: 36
Trinitarian Congregational Church:
  76
Trolley: xiii, 32
Troy (N.Y.): 3

*Ulmus americana*: see under Elm
Underground Railroad: 83
Union Turnpike: 35
United Nations: xiii, 21–22, 30–33
United Nations Site Committee: 31,
  32, 33
United States Congress: 10, 31
University of Massachusetts: 36
University of Michigan: 11
University of Wisconsin: 68

Values, community: xi, 19, 21, 62, 69
Vanzetti, Bartolomeo: 68
Vaux, Calvert: 90
Virginia Road: 21, 22, 39–42
Vital records: 5, 63, 64, 72

W., A. M.: see under Whiting, Anna
  Maria
Walden Pond: 19–20, 32
Walden Pond amusement park: see
  under Fitchburg Railroad
Walden Pond State Reservation: 1, 21
Walden Street: 20, 52, 53
Walker, William: 31
Watertown (Mass.): 9, 63, 64
Watts, C. F.: 93
Wayland (Mass.): 33
Wayside: 93
"We gather together to ask the Lord's
  blessing": 78

Webster, Daniel: 13
Welfare, public: xii, xiv, 37–58; see
  also under Philanthropy
West Church: 53
West Concord: 20, 51
West Concord Shopping Plaza: 20
Westford (Mass.): 9
Wheeler, Richard Warren: 22
Wheeler, Ruth Robinson: xiii, 32, 65
  *Concord: Climate for Freedom*:
  xiii
Wheeler, Wilfrid: 22, 24
Wheeler-Minot House: see under
  Thoreau birthplace
Whipping Post Elm: 2, 13–17, 35
Whiting, Anna Maria: 43–45, 83
Whiting, Louisa: 83
Whiting, William: 33, 43
Whitney, Ellen Frances: 49
Widow's thirds: 38, 39–42
William Munroe Special Collections:
  see under Concord Free Public
  Library
Williamsburg: see under Colonial
  Williamsburg
Woburn (Mass.): 9, 92
Women's Parish Association: see
  under First Parish in Concord
Wood, Charles G.: 28
World War I: 68

Yalta: 31
Yankee Freemen Movement: 68
*Yeoman's Gazette*: 4
Young, B. Loring: 11

Zoning by-law (1928): 20